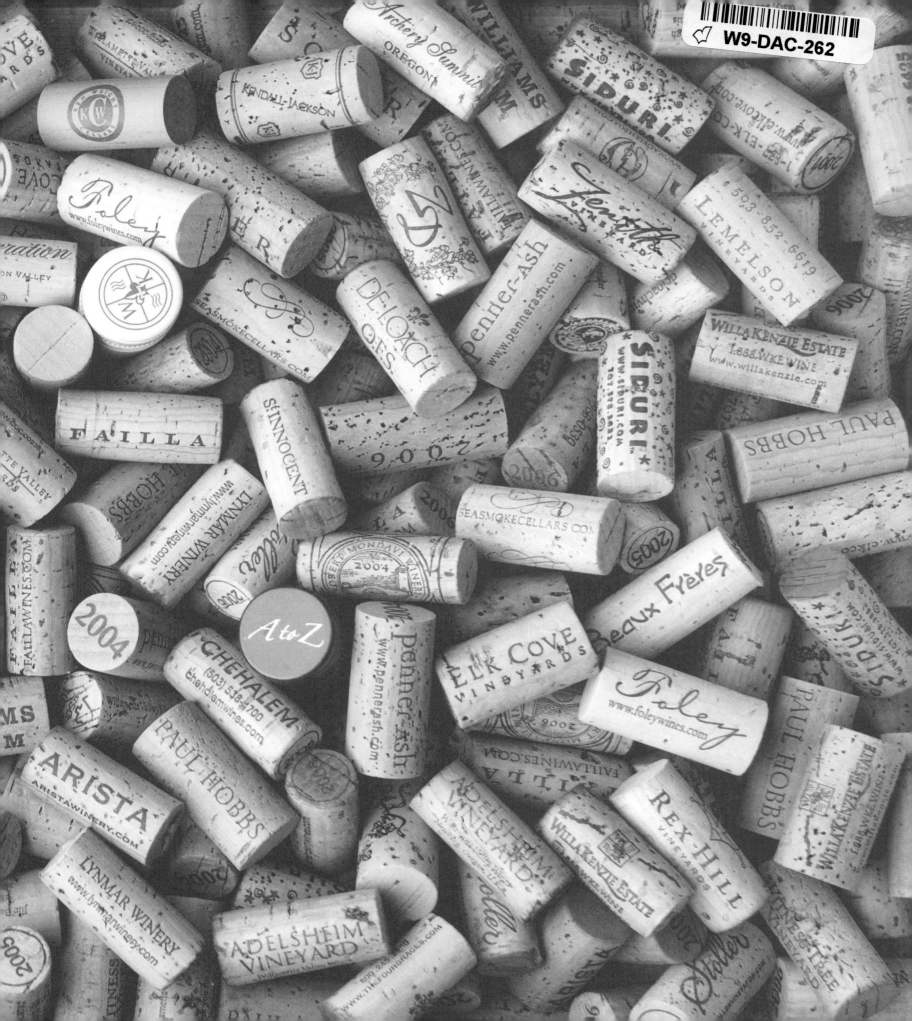

PASSION *for* PINOT

PASSION *for* PINOT

A Journey Through America's Pinot Noir Country

Drink more Pinot!

Photography by **ANDREA JOHNSON** & **ROBERT HOLMES**   Text by **JORDAN MACKAY**

Foreword by **ERIC ASIMOV**

TEN SPEED PRESS

Berkeley | Toronto

Ten Speed Press
PO Box 7123
Berkeley, California 94707
www.tenspeed.com

Distributed in Australia by Simon and Schuster Australia, in Canada by
Ten Speed Press Canada, in New Zealand by Southern Publishers Group,
in South Africa by Real Books, and in the United Kingdom and Europe
by Publishers Group UK.

Produced by Carpe Diem Books®
Project coordinator: Ross Eberman
Design: theBookDesigners
Copyediting: Tina Caputo
Cartography: Ben Pease
Index: Maria Sosnowski
Manufacturing: Dick Owsiany

Printed in China
First printing, 2009

1 2 3 4 5 6 7 8 9 10 — 13 12 11 10 09

Contents

Taking a barrel sample at Paul Hobbs Winery.

FOREWORD

GRAPE GROWING AND WINEMAKING have come a long way in the last fifty years. Visit any winery and you'll find enough test tubes, gauges and laboratory equipment to make you look around for the guys in the white coats. Winemakers toss around words like polyphenols, clones and oenocyanins and debate the merits of reverse osmosis and micro-oxygenation. Yet as hard as we try to turn winemaking into a science, the climate, the soil and those pesky vitis vinifera grapes refuse to knuckle under to human control.

Of all the grapes that are transformed into fine wine, none are as steadfast as Pinot Noir in refusing to be tamed. As a result, winemakers have their own vocabulary for describing the grape: difficult, finicky, elusive, temperamental and my favorite, femme fatale. If any grape would be at home in the pose of the femme fatale—smoke curling from its lips, long, irresistible legs crossed as another winemaker is sent to his doom—it would be Pinot Noir.

Yet if anything, the difficulties posed by the Pinot Noir grape are meaningless, for its allure compels winemakers simply to try harder. If it requires settling on Mount Harlan in the middle of nowhere, without electricity and running water, so that the Pinot Noir vines can be planted on limestone soil, well, then that's what it takes. Or maybe it's your idea of fun to live in a tent off a dirt road on the wildly beautiful but rugged Sonoma Coast so that you can plant a vineyard that maybe—just maybe—will ripen each year?

The stories of hardships and singular visions abound, whether in the Santa Rita Hills or the Santa Cruz Mountains, the Santa Maria Valley or the Willamette Valley, and so often they begin with an obsession with Pinot Noir. And more often than not, this obsession begins as an obsession with Burgundy.

No other wine is as treasured as fine red Burgundy, named for the land where the mystique of Pinot Noir was born and nurtured. Of course, the Burgundians have had the benefit of a millennium to determine all the best sites for planting Pinot Noir in their sliver of a valley. In the United States the work is going on right before our eyes.

And so, what you see here in the gorgeous photographs of Robert Holmes and Andrea Johnson, and what you will read about in the lively, spirited prose of Jordan Mackay, is not the triumphal ending to a great success story (although you may disagree with that assessment when you taste some of the wines). It is rather a snapshot of a work in progress, of an attempt to come to grips with a grape and a wine that are endlessly frustrating because they can be so thoroughly, joyously enchanting.

No matter which new clones of Pinot Noir are planted in which types of soil and monitored by which sorts of gauges and transformed into wine by which sorts of contraptions, Pinot Noir will always have its way. To paraphrase the wine writer Hugh Johnson, great Pinot Noirs do not make statements, they pose questions. *Passion for Pinot* may not resolve those questions, but it amply demonstrates why winemakers keep searching for answers.

Eric Asimov
Chief Wine Critic
The New York Times

Dawn over snowy winter scene at Bella Vida Vineyard, Dundee Hills, Oregon.

A PERFECT STORM OF PINOT

W E WERE STANDING IN A VINEYARD bathed in delicate spring sunshine. Its luminance covered the crest of a knob-like hill, contrasting the dark, brooding shoulders of Oregon's Coast Range, which towered nearby. Looking at the young Pinot Noir vines, with their newly sprouted leaves reaching eagerly toward the sun, the Oregon winemaker, Kelley Fox (of Scott Paul Wines), asked, "What's the old saying—'You know you're on to something when you get ridiculed'?" She was addressing Mo Momtazi, the Pinot's owner, who was relating the story of the conversion of his vineyard to the controversial system of biodynamic farming. One of his reasons for making the conversion was to try to save this very section of Pinot Noir, a weak area of land that hadn't displayed enough strength to ripen the grapes. "There were a lot of skeptics, a lot of people who wondered," Momtazi said, about the feasibility of farming his enormous vineyard, 95% Pinot, biodynamically, making it one of the largest such Pinot Noir vineyards in the world. In just a few years under the new method (composting, zero chemical inputs) his success is evident not only in his own richly colored, deeply flavored

Pinots under his Maysara label, but in the twenty or so other Pinots made by all the people who buy his fruit.

Words like ridicule, doubt and risk come up frequently in tales of this perplexing grape. For years, the pursuit of Pinot Noir—unproven, unpredictable, uneconomical—was seen as folly on the grandest scale. Yet, Pinot is seductive in ways that other grapes are not, its elusive beauty leading to irresistible attraction. As wine critic Jancis Robinson has written, "It leads us a terrible dance, tantalizing with an occasional glimpse of the riches in store for those who persevere, yet obstinately refusing to be tamed."

Such was the experience of Andre Tchelistcheff, the revered Napa winemaker who claimed that the 1946 Beaulieu Pinot Noir was one of the greatest wines he had made in his life. And, despite 48 years of trying, he died in 1994 having never replicated it. As he famously proclaimed, "God made Cabernet Sauvignon, whereas the devil made Pinot Noir."

Like so many beauties of literature—from sirens and mermaids to Lolita—that have led characters to their demise, the pursuit of Pinot Noir more than any other grape has inspired risky behavior. But, more often than not—at least in America—submission to the siren song has transformed lives for the better. The hero may have had to endure ridicule, skepticism, doubt and risk along the way, but the results cannot be denied.

Consider the doubt Josh Jensen inspired among family, friends, and investors when in the early 1970s his search for limestone soil on which to plant Pinot Noir (paralleling the ground of Burgundy) led him to a purchase a remote, desiccated rock mountain in a remote, sparsely populated section of California's Central Coast. Bucking drought, the elements, and the intransigence of solid rock, Jensen has made some of this country's greatest Pinots under his Calera label, indeed some of the finest ever made outside of France.

Not far away, Gary Pisoni endured ridicule for his decision to plant Pinot Noir in the benchland above the Salinas Valley. Known as "America's Salad Bowl," the Salinas Valley is some of the most productive farmland in the nation and thus not typically associated with quality wine. While some grape vines grew there before Pisoni arrived, they tended to be unripe Cabernet Sauvignon and Merlot. But thanks to Pisoni's strange vision, what were once just rugged hillsides overlooking rich asparagus and broccoli fields are now the source of some of the most sought-after Pinot grapes in California.

Ditto David Lett, known as "Papa Pinot," whose decision to try planting Pinot Noir in Oregon's Willamette Valley was originally disparaged by his professors at the University of California at Davis. We know how that turned out.

These anecdotes are not by any means offered to suggest that planting Pinot Noir is any longer a fool's errand. Rather, they are meant to illustrate the compulsion, the near religious fervor that Pinot Noir can birth in people's souls. No grape has engendered so many stories of life transformation. No wine has so compelled people to suddenly uproot and dramatically change their lives.

Take winemaker Jamie Kutch, of Kutch Wines in San Francisco. For him a single bottle of Russian River Valley Pinot Noir was not only a wine, but also a summons—one that a few years ago he answered. A Wall Street trader at the time, Kutch was very into wine and drank a lot of it. It was, however, the taste of a single Pinot Noir, a 2002 Kosta-Browne Kanzler Vineyard, that caused him within weeks of the fateful taste to quit his job and move to California to make Pinot Noir himself. Still intoxicated less than a year later during harvest, he sent a diamond ring (in a box) down the conveyer amid the clusters of ripe Pinot Noir to his girlfriend of eight years who was sorting the fruit at the bottom. After the next harvest's fermentations were completed, they honeymooned in Thailand.

Consider the story of Deb and Bill Hatcher. Visiting the Willamette Valley from St. Louis in 1985, they sampled wine at The Eyrie Vineyards and Adelsheim Vineyard. "It was love at first taste," Deb recalls. She was thirty-five at the time. Nevertheless, within three weeks they had quit their jobs, packed up and moved to Oregon. Both worked their first harvests that year. Now they own two brands, A to Z and Rex Hill Vineyards, and are, with their partners, the largest wine producers in Oregon.

Or take the example of Steve and Carol Girard, who owned one of the hottest Cabernet labels in the Napa Valley in the mid-'80s. Unbeknownst to the Cabernet, they had for several years been conducting a discreet but impassioned affair with Pinot Noir. Ultimately unable to stand their double-life, they sold their winery and their name and excused themselves from the sunny life of Napa, buying an unglamorous 2,000-acre sheep farm under the more tortured skies of Oregon's central Willamette Valley. The sheep farm became Benton-Lane Winery.

I believe the epigram Kelley Fox was trying to remember that day in the vineyard comes from Oscar Wilde: "Ridicule is the tribute paid to the genius by the mediocrities." I'm sure none of the people cited

Wide open vista of Los Carneros vineyards.

After harvest the Goldeneye vineyards of the Anderson Valley turn to gold.

above and the many others whose lives have been transformed by Pinot Noir would call themselves geniuses. And certainly none would take such a bitter tone in describing their work. Rather, I think, they would say that all the genius is in Pinot Noir itself and that they are the ones merrily paying tribute.

THE TIME IS NOW

PINOT NOIR IS SEEING ITS GREATEST ever popularity in the United States. According to Nielsen Company research, in the two years between May 2006 and May 2008 sales of Pinot jumped an astonishing 36%. Each year Pinot sales grew by around 20% over the year before, making it the fastest growing red variety in the country.

A seismic 18% jump in typically staid grocery store sales between October 24, 2004 and July 2, 2005 confirmed the trend. The significance of October 2004 is not lost on Pinot lovers. That is the month the movie *Sideways* was released. Though the bittersweet, tragicomic movie focused on a couple of complicated and generally unsavory characters, one could say that Pinot Noir was the supporting player. Taking place predominantly among the vineyards of California's south Central Coast, the film set its drama in a world of wine tasting and discussion. At one point, the main character Miles says of Pinot Noir, "Oh its flavors, they're just the most haunting and brilliant and thrilling and subtle and . . . ancient on the planet."

Seeing characters, no matter how humiliating and self-destructive their actions might be, take such pleasure and interest in wine (much less Pinot) was thirst-inducing for many Americans. Remarkable was the asymmetrical effect it had on Pinot sales. While the movie was a surprise hit and won an Oscar for

Best Adapted Screenplay, it nevertheless was a so-called Independent film and had nowhere near the box office numbers of, say, a Spielberg blockbuster. The relatively small audience, compared to its enormous impact on the sales of a particular wine, leads me to believe that rather than causing the Pinot Noir explosion, *Sideways* was merely the catalyst, the match thrown on a great pile of fuel. In a wine environment that favored bigger and in which most of the wines being hailed by retailers and the press weren't particularly versatile or friendly with food, Pinot Noir—lighter bodied and food friendly—was that fuel so ready to be ignited.

A LITTLE BACKGROUND

A POSSIBLE REASON FOR THE TANTALIZING and fugitive nature of Pinot's beauty is that, as grape varieties go, it is one of the most ancient. Like other very old organisms (whales, platypuses), Pinot Noir is replete with mystery. Some of the earliest recorded descriptions of a vine resembling Pinot Noir appear in the first century of the Common Era, suggesting that its history likely dates back much further. Some speculate that Pinot Noir is one of the earliest wild grape vines domesticated by man. And if you have experience raising a wolf puppy adopted from the wild—or even just a stray cat—you understand the unpredictable and often unfathomable behavior that results from intelligence and instinct we don't fully understand. Pinot Noir, which we have been domesticating for at least 2,000 years, stubbornly retains its wily, opaque personality.

Pinot is the great red grape of Burgundy (and Champagne) and is considered one of the world's "noble" varieties alongside the likes of Cabernet Sauvignon, Chardonnay and Riesling. In Burgundy,

Moving barrels at Clos du Val in Napa Valley.

it makes some of the world's most sought-after wines, wines so hip that we just call them by name: La Tâche and Musigny, for instance. Of course, out of Pinot Noir, Burgundy also makes plenty of more humble reds of the Tuesday-night variety.

While there is no proof as to exactly how or when Pinot Noir first came to America, it's pretty clear that the grape arrived in the middle years of the 19th century. Evidence for its existence is strong through the 1880s and 1890s, when a mania took hold in California for growing as many of the diverse varieties of Europe as possible. Pinot Noir was undoubtedly a part of early California viticulture, but the challenges of growing and vinifying it combined

with the overwhelming fame of Bordeaux relegated it to an exceedingly minor place. Despite the fact it was regarded with a sanguine attitude in some wine circles, Pinot-Noir-based wines between the 1890s and the repeal of Prohibition in 1933 largely fell into a void. Indeed, Prohibition severely derailed the evolution of American wine in general.

After Prohibition it still took another two generations for Pinot to find its foothold. While Cabernet Sauvignon ascended as California's most prominent red variety, Pinot Noir was being made, albeit in very small quantities, right beside it by most of the major producers. Quality seems to have severely lagged, though, as reports describe wines

Historic log of the first Pinot harvest at Hanzell Vinyards in 1956.

that were oxidized, herbaceous, lacking color and otherwise unpleasant. According to John Hager's indispensable book *North American Pinot Noir*, the unfortunate quality of those Pinots likely resulted from crude winemaking technique. At that time most red wines were made using a uniform, brusque process that, while acceptable for tougher varieties like Cab and Zinfandel, was perilous for Pinot. It would be like a chef employing the same touch when making both sausage and soufflé. Many well-known Napa brands—Caymus, Sterling, Louis Martini and others—stopped producing it altogether. As Hager writes, the message was clear: "Pinot Noir could not be made well in

the New World, it was said—and repeated—over and over." Witness the birth of an underdog.

As is the case with most underdogs, the hopeful and stubborn pushed back. A response was brewing in the collective consciousness of disparate individuals, all Burgundy lovers, who felt that with proper care, Pinot Noir could flourish. Theirs were small operations, the products of individual effort and inspiration, rather than strategic corporate expansion. It started with a vineyard called Hanzell, specializing in Pinot Noir and Chardonnay, planted by James Zellerbach in 1952 in the hills above the town of Sonoma. (Early on, the Chardonnay fared better than the Pinot, which had its first vintage in

Harvest at Bergstrom estate vineyard, Oregon.

Anderson Valley harvest in the Goldeneye vineyards

Judging in progress at a Mendocino wine competition.

1956. However, the early Pinots were, and still are distinguished. I recently tasted a 1968 Hanzell that was remarkably youthful and delicious.) In the mid-1960s, Chalone began production from an old vineyard in the desolate foothills of the Pinnacles Range outside the town of Soledad in California's Salinas Valley. Joe Rochioli planted Pinot in the Russian River Valley in 1968.

In 1966, David Lett, smitten by Pinot and looking for a climate similar to Burgundy, moved to Oregon's Willamette Valley and planted its first acres. Within a decade, he was producing wines that were competing with top Burgundies at blind tasting competitions in France. He was, over the course of the next decade, joined by other Pinot lovers Dick Erath, Dick Ponzi, Myron Redford, Bill Blosser and Susan Sokol Blosser, and David Adelsheim. Likewise, in the 1970s other inspired Pinot operations such as Calera, Carneros Creek, Husch, Navarro and Sanford settled up and down the California coast. These first seeds were all it took to create the vast Pinot Noir garden we have today.

Geese fly over King Estate vineyard in Lorane Valley, southwest of Eugene, Oregon.

THOUGHTS ABOUT
THE GRAPE AND THE WINE

"PINOT NOIR, MORE THAN ANYTHING, should tell the truth," says Scott Wright, founder of Oregon's Scott Paul Wines. "And it does that very well. But you have to take a risk in order to hear the truth and then you might not always get what you expect."

Pinot's reputation for confounding and frustrating even its most ardent fans is well deserved. Indeed, along with its truth-telling comes a bewil-dering propensity to speak in riddles, to defy conventional wisdom, and to willfully stray from the best-laid plans.

"You never know exactly what you're going to get," says Tony Soter of Soter Vineyards. As we walk his beautiful hilltop vineyard off of Mineral Springs Road in Oregon, he says, "With thirty years of experience, we didn't know when we planted here how well it would turn out. We hoped. We believed. But it's like having a kid—you put everything in place, give it what it needs and then sit on the edge of your seat, waiting to see it develop a personality." Sometimes it works out wonderfully, as it has so far for Soter's young vineyard.

And sometimes, success can be elusive, as with Josh Jensen's most recent planting at Calera—a small strip of vineyard that connects two well-established and hallowed single vineyards. "We call it our problem child," says Jensen, confiding that the wines from the new plot have been aggressively tannic.

"We can't figure out why it's turning out this way. The soil and exposure are the same as the neighboring vineyards." That's unpredictable Pinot Noir in a nutshell. The vineyard is only a few years old, though, and Jensen, with his decades of experience will no doubt bring it around.

"Fickle" is often the word used to describe Pinot Noir in the vineyard. As the character Miles cogently observes in *Sideways*, "It's thin-skinned,

Hawk flies over Sea Smoke vineyard, Sta. Rita Hills, California.

Kendall-Jackson's Falk Vineyard in the Anderson Valley glimpsed through an old barn.

Relaxing with Pinot at the end of the day.

temperamental, ripens early. Pinot needs constant care and attention." While all this is true, says Victor Gallegos of Sea Smoke Cellars (whose wine had a cameo in *Sideways)* in California's Santa Barbara County, "What's most important to remember is that like a person it reacts to everything you do, both in the winery and out. You have to make sure you think about exactly how you're going to act and then perform every action gently and precisely."

Pinot Noir can be as perplexing in the bottle as it is in the vineyard. While the general description of Pinot Noir wine usually includes words like *silky, elegant* and *feminine,* in practice you'll find all sorts of styles—from massive and tannic to delicate and light. Pinot can be bewildering during its maturation in the bottle as well—shutting down one month, blossoming the next, and then shutting down again. As Mark Vlossak, of St. Innocent Winery in Oregon's Eola Hills, says, "You never know how a bottle of Pinot's going to be showing at any point in its life. You can only open it and hope."

Clearly a vital trait for the intrepid grower of Pinot Noir, hope, as we shall see, when combined with ingenuity, care and hard work, can yield stunning results.

Vines shut down after harvest, turning brilliant yellow, Willamette Valley, Oregon.

Perfectly formed cluster of ripe Pinot Noir, Willamette Valley, Oregon.

Old barrels wait for recycling at DeLoach Vineyards.

A quiet corner in Chehalem's barrel room.

On the question of Burgundy

More than once during tastings I've heard irritated winemakers say, "I'm not trying to make Burgundy—I'm trying to make the best (fill in your favorite Oregon or California AVA) Pinot Noir I can." But then a moment later they'll turn around and say something like, "This one is very Burgundian," or "It reminds me of a Gevrey-Chambertin." In the course of a few minutes they've perfectly dramatized America's tortured relationship to Burgundy.

Pinot Noir, the grape, comes from Burgundy, as does our sense of what its wine should taste like. Much like an over-achieving older sibling in the eyes of an adoring younger one, the example Burgundy sets is source of both inspiration and anxiety for New World Pinot Noir.

Here, as always, retaining a sense of perspective is paramount. We must remember that Burgundy has centuries of experience to our decades. The grape has most likely evolved to perform in the Burgundian soil and climate, which is altogether different than ours. Furthermore, Burgundy's wines have defined the category of Pinot Noir, making following suit difficult. And all of this is complicated further by our tendency toward selective memory.

When we invoke a comparison with Burgundy we tend to mean only its greatest hits, while turning a blind eye to its (many, many) duds.

The clichéd distinctions between Burgundy and New World Pinot Noir have the former as being more earthy, acidic and structured with the latter being more fruit-forward, alcoholic and round. While providing a serviceable guideline, I've seen these distinctions break down at blind tastings so often as to render the term "Burgundian" almost meaningless. The great wines of Burgundy are indeed an inspiration, but need not be a prescription.

"Great wines don't make statements, they pose questions. To end with an exclamation mark is easy; when a question mark, perhaps not more difficult, but far more interesting."

—HUGH JOHNSON

Fog rolls in the valley below Penner-Ash winery, Yamhill-Carlton, Oregon.

2 TERROIR

THE HARDEST QUESTION TO ANSWER about any wine is, Why does it taste that way? The answer comes primarily in the form of a single word, though the word is the most complicated, slippery and controversial in the wine world: *terroir*. A French coinage closely associated with Pinot Noir, *terroir* is commonly described as the total growing environment of the grape vine, including soil composition, exposition, climate, weather, elevation and any other metric one can think of by which to measure or characterize a vineyard site. But to answer a question about a wine by answering *"terroir"* is somewhat akin to throwing up one's hands and saying, "I don't know," because definitive understanding of how a site's complex climatic features affect a grapevine is still largely beyond our grasp. And because of this inscrutability giant tankers of ink have been spilled in argument not just about what constitutes *terroir*, but about how important it is, whether human beings should be factored into the definition, and whether it even exists.

Of course, *terroir*, in its most basic sense, exists. Writ large, this is obvious when comparing, say, a

Shiraz from Australia's Barossa Valley with a Syrah from Côte Rôtie. The same grape grown in entirely different environments produces wines that taste nothing alike. What sets Pinot Noir apart from most grapes is that, if a wine can be read as a kind of description of a particular place, Pinot is a very acute and meticulous reporter. It can meter differences not just between hemispheres, but also between adjacent plots on the same slope. The questions we must ask ourselves are: How do we recognize such differences, and are they important?

With regard to the first question, there is some confusion as to what *terroir* tastes like. This stems from the fact that it doesn't necessarily take the form of a taste—it's more of a feel. The more we try to pin *terroir* down with language, the more fleeting it becomes. Sometimes it can be reduced to a particular characteristic—minerality, say, or a certain lushness of tannin—which is most easily recognized by its recurrence in wines from the same vineyard made by different producers. But sometimes we might perceive what the French call the *gout de terroir*—a sense of place—in a wine from a vineyard that we've never tasted before. That perception is of what the brilliant critic (and Oregon resident) Matt Kramer famously coined "somewhereness," a sense that the wine comes from somewhere as opposed to just anywhere. There is something

Horses and cows graze next to vineyards at WillaKenzie Estate, Yamhill-Carlton, Oregon.

instantly compelling about a wine with somewhereness, and Pinot Noir, when well made, is one of the best grapes at communicating this.

As to the second question, Jean-Charles Boisset, owner of both Boisset International in Burgundy and DeLoach in California's Russian River Valley, is unstinting. He told me in his perfect, French-accented English, "Pinot Noir is the most sensitive of grapes. When you find a specific place that makes exceptional Pinot Noir it is your duty to work with that vineyard and wine so that it can give voice to this place. Not every grape has this ability, so when there is the opportunity you must take it."

As a Burgundian, Boisset was born into the mindset that the wine grape's purpose is to express the nature of the land on which it was grown. To take his analogy, if a wine is the voice, the land is the song. This way of thinking is novel to many of us, because much of the history of American wine has celebrated the singer, not the song: i.e. we ask simply for a glass of Chardonnay, not a glass of white southern Sonoma Coast. This is changing, however. And, because of its sensitivity to place, Pinot Noir is today helping to bring the focus back to the song.

Many places within California and Oregon have been discovered to make good music with Pinot Noir. Being definitive about the distinguishing features of

Sheep graze on Tony Soter's Mineral Springs Vineyard overlooking Lemelson's Stermer vineyard, Yamhill-Carlton, Oregon.

the Pinot grape is impossible, as the elusiveness of *terroir* will continue to dog us. With that in mind, this chapter humbly offers a sketch of each great West Coast Pinot region in the hope that a slightly greater understanding of the place will increase our enjoyment of its wine.

For simplicity's sake, the chapter is organized by AVA, American Viticultural Area, which is a designated winegrowing region as defined by the U.S. government. While convenient as a way to differentiate regions, AVAs are less a precise delineation of soils or indication of wine character and more, as Matt Kramer calls it, "simple fence building." They are almost without exception too big. Being oversized, the AVAs lose their effectiveness in corralling, organizing and describing wines. But, that's okay. It's still early in the game of defining regions, however the maps on the forthcoming pages help reference these AVAs and their geographical relationships to one another.

OREGON

OREGON IS IN A COMMITTED RELATIONSHIP with Pinot Noir. In California, it was, until recently, an afterthought or curiosity, but Pinot Noir is the love of Oregon's life, its *raison d'etre*, accounting for almost 75% of its total planted vineyard land. The affair began in the mid-1960s, when Oregon became a sort of a refugee camp for stateless Pinot Noir lovers. Disenfranchised by the wine establishment in California, where many of them lived, they had been told that the Golden State was too warm to grow Pinot Noir and that Oregon was too cold and wet to ripen wine grapes of any kind. A couple of visionaries, however, steadfastly refused to listen. David Lett and Charles Coury had done the climate

research and decided that in Oregon not only was Pinot possible, but that it was a better answer than California. (Lett, by the way, gets more of the credit today, because he stuck with it; Coury closed up shop in 1977.)

The refugee camp soon became a sort of promised land for Pinot lovers, as the likes of Dick Erath and Dick Ponzi, both Californians, soon followed, as well as Myron Redford of Amity Vineyards. Another wave soon materialized with the arrival of other important Pinot-philes like the Sokol-Blossers and David Adelsheim. The explosion has continued unabated. In the eight years between 1973 and 1981, the number of wineries grew from seven to thirty-five. Twenty years later there were 156 wineries, and by 2007 that number had more than doubled to 393. While most of the Pinot Noir growing has focused on the northern end of the Willamette Valley, other suitable regions for the grape, yet to be discovered or fully realized, exist. But for the purposes of this overview, I will focus on the particular nature of the Willamette Valley, as it is the beating heart of Oregon Pinot Noir.

WILLAMETTE VALLEY

A LONG, WIDE VALLEY REACHING more than 100 miles from northwest of Portland to a few miles past Eugene, the Willamette Valley AVA, created in 1983, is framed on its western edge by the Coast Range and on the eastern edge by the Cascades. Green and lush, the Willamette has some of the richest farmland in the nation, which, of course, is no good for wine, as grapevines perform better when life is not too easy. Therefore, almost all the vineyards are planted overlooking the valley on hillsides where the soils are thinner.

The climate is cool and Pacific Northwestern, meaning it's subjected to buckets of rain over the course of the long dark winter, fall and spring. Weather comes in from the Pacific Ocean over the irregular peaks of the low-lying Coast Range and more urgently through a break in the range known as the Van Duzer Corridor. Rain occasionally arrives early, disrupting the harvest, as it does frequently in Burgundy. However, more like California and less like Burgundy, the Willamette sees little to no rain during the summer months—Pinot's prime growing season. Therefore, some irrigate their grapevines during the hot, rainless summers. Others, however, refrain, saying it's unnecessary and preferring the wine made from dry-farmed grapes.

Vineyard soils come mainly in two broad flavor categories: marine sediment and volcanic basalt. The former is the result of uplifted ancient seabeds thrust to the surface by plate tectonics and taking the form of silty clay and loams, typically overlaying sandstone. The latter is the residue of both epic lava flows and volcanic burbling through the sedimentary rock. Some places show a purity of one soil type, while in other places they are mixed. There are, of course, variants with each type, and vintners are only recently becoming highly sensitive to these implications. A third soil, Laurelwood, is sort of a combination of the two, composed of volcanic ash mixed with wind-blown loess.

Significantly, the 45th parallel, considered a harmonious latitude for ripening grapes, shoots through the Willamette Valley. The higher latitude, compared to California, means that during the growing season, the Willamette Valley experiences up to two or three more hours of daylight each day. This prolonged exposure is cited by some as key to Oregon's success. "I taste flavors and qualities at lower sugar levels here in Oregon that I would never taste at the same stage in

Four Graces Black Family Estate vineyards, Dundee Hills, Oregon.

Archery Summit estate vineyard, Dundee Hills AVA, Oregon.

Stoller estate vineyards overlooking the family's original turkey farm in Dayton, Dundee Hills, Oregon.

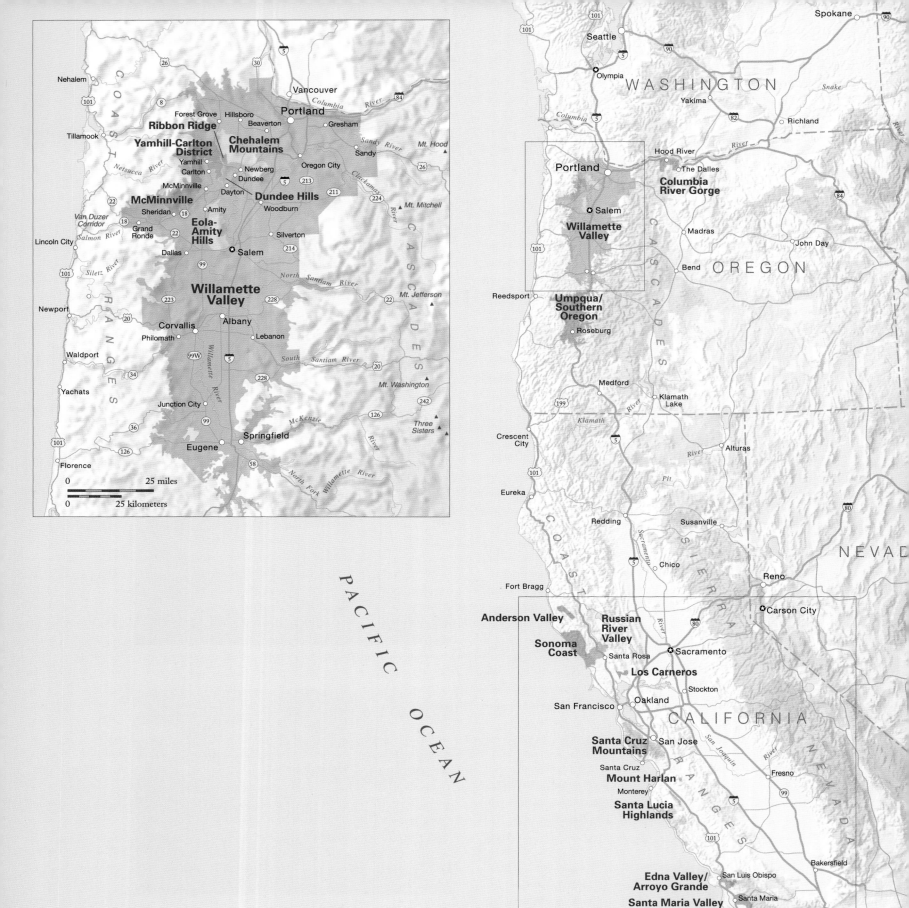

Mt. Hood is clearly visible from many vineyards of the Dundee Hills, Oregon.

Winter snow over dormant Pinot Noir vines at WillaKenzie Estate vineyard, Yamhill-Carlton AVA, Willamette Valley, Oregon.

California," says Tony Soter of Soter Vineyards, who has made admirable wines in both places.

Six AVAs contained completely inside the larger Willamette Valley AVA were created in 2005 and 2006. A wine label can thus bear the name of the specific sub-AVA from which it comes or the catchall Willamette Valley AVA, or both. The six AVAs are all clustered at the northern end of the Willamette and almost all take the form of hills rising from the flat valley floor like islands in a sea, making them easily discernible on a map and giving them an intuitive, visual legitimacy. The fact that these sub-AVAs are distinct on a map, however, does not necessarily find correlation in the wines. Discerning the differences among wines from each of the appellations in blind tastings is not easy, as young vines, a uniformity of clones and a vast diversity of winemaking styles all help to blur the differences. Over time, though, unique characteristics of each region may emerge.

CHEHALEM MOUNTAINS

STRETCHING 20 MILES AND encompassing 68,000 acres, the Chehalem Mountains are a large, sometimes brooding mass of hills at the northeastern end of the Willamette Valley wine country. Forming a bulwark between the other AVAs and the Tualatin Valley to the north, the Chehalem Mountains feature vineyards planted as low as 200 feet and up into the hills at elevations between 800 and 1,000 feet. Exposures vary, but most vineyards are planted on the southwest-facing side of the mountains.

As a wine area, the Chehalem Mountains region has both historical import and cutting-edge relevance. It was in this area that David Adelsheim planted in 1971, making his the second vineyard in the area (the first was one of David Erath's). Highly regarded for both his advocacy of the Chehalem Mountains AVA and the Oregon wine industry in general, Adelsheim gave me a brief tutorial on Chehalem Mountains geology one typically rainy spring day at his winery.

"We now know that the Chehalem Mountains is a borderline between the very old marine sedimentary soils that predominate to the west of here and the much younger basaltic lava flow that issued from the eastern part of the state and flowed west," he said. "So we have both main soils here." Located on the western side, Adelsheim's estate vineyard is composed of the marine sediment, which he showed me by rushing outside and pulling a hard, but friable piece of rock from a pit behind his winery. "This stuff drains wonderfully," he said, cracking a piece in his hand. Adelsheim's hair may have grayed, but he moves around his winery with a spry bounce in his step. His wines today could be characterized similarly—they have a lightness and energy, but a sense of solidity as well.

Less than a mile away, however, Deborah Hatcher of Rex Hill showed me her gem of a Chehalem Mountain AVA vineyard, Jacob-Hart, which lies on volcanic soil. "You might want to knock all the red dirt off your boots before getting back in the car," she said.

A third soil, called Laurelwood, crops up here and there as well. Well-known examples of this soil are found in Ponzi's two prized Chehalem Mountains vineyards, Abetina and Madrona, located on the eastern face of the mountains at about 600 feet. Laurelwood appears clear on the other side of the mountains at Chehalem Vineyards' Corral Creek site.

These days the Chehalem Mountains AVA is generating a lot of interest for new vineyard development. With its rare profusion (or confusion) of different soil types, variety of exposures and altitudes, it's

Domaine Drouhin's gravity flow winery design is evident from this aerial view, Dundee Hills, Oregon.

Chehalem's Coral Creek Vineyards, Chehalem Mountains, Oregon.

attractive for people looking to expand their holdings. Seemingly everyone I talked with has some sort of new site in the works up there.

RIBBON RIDGE

IN FRONT OF A LARGE AUDIENCE at a Pinot Noir seminar not long ago, Mike Etzel of Beaux Frères Vineyards & Winery, which lies in the appellation, described the Ribbon Ridge AVA as being shaped like "a turd." He got laughs, but I'll never be able to look at the AVA again without that image coming to mind. In spite of the lowly comparison, the tiny region is home to some standout vineyards.

Just west of the Chehalem Mountains and technically located within that AVA, the self-contained island of uplifted marine sediment known as Ribbon Ridge first achieved prominence thanks to Harry Peterson-Nedry's Ridgecrest Vineyard, planted there in 1980. While not big—just over 3 miles long and almost a mile wide—the AVA is chock full of notable properties such as Beaux Frères, Patricia Green Cellars and Brick House, which have made names for themselves with excellent, though stylistically diverse, wines.

Beaux Frères is known for rich and deep wines, while Patricia Green makes Pinot Noir of exceptional grace. And Doug Tunnell, the man behind Brick House, makes biodynamic, dry-farmed wines notable for their delicious Old-World earthiness.

YAMHILL-CARLTON

ASK ANYONE IN THE WILLAMETTE VALLEY to describe the Yamhill-Carlton District and they'll likely defer, mumbling something to the effect of, "You should talk to Ken Wright." Wright, the spirited, intense and celebrated winemaker, has achieved notoriety for the creation of three highly successful wine brands—Panther Creek, Domaine Serene and Ken Wright Cellars—and is thought to have somewhat of a magic touch. He makes a passionate case for the potential of the soils and climate of his district of choice, Yamhill-Carlton, so it's natural to seek him out for a regional tour.

"Yamhill-Carlton is composed mainly of ancient marine sedimentary soils," he told me as we stood atop a hill called Savannah Ridge at his Abbott Claim Vineyard, a site which Wright is convinced is one of

Chehelam's Ridgecrest Vineyards, Ribbon Ridge, Oregon.

the best in the valley. "Up here, we've got a variant called Wellsdale and you can see its red, brown and yellowish colored soils. The soil drains pretty well," he added, "and it's less than 3 feet down to mother rock. Typical of the area, the wine shows darker fruit character, as opposed to the red fruit you find on volcanic soils."

From Savannah Ridge we could look west to the Coast Range, which, Wright said, provides a rain shadow for the Yamhill-Carlton District. "Once the rain gets over the Coast Range it tends to keep going, stopping and dropping on the next feature it meets, the Dundee Hills." Wright was kind enough to share his Savannah Ridge discovery with Tony Soter. Soter made his Pinot reputation in California's Carneros region with a brand called Etude, but returned to his childhood home of Oregon to launch Soter Vineyards. His Mineral Springs estate is very close to Wright's Abbott Claim, and side-by-side comparisons of the two wines will make for interesting investigations into the nature of *terroir*. While the wines have different winemaking and different clones (Soter nurtured and brought with him an heirloom clone he discovered in California), the vineyard conditions are almost identical.

Savannah Ridge anchors the southeastern part of the district, but there's much more to see. As the name implies, the AVA is formed of the hills that wrap around the low-lying towns of Carlton and, to its north, Yamhill. The region's ring of vineyards make a horseshoe shape that follows eastern foothills of the Coast Range up and around the town of Yamhill and back south on the hills east (only including land between the elevations of 200 and 1,000 feet) of the towns, with flat valley land in the middle. The town of Carlton is a growing wine village, boasting several wineries and tasting rooms, including the Carlton Winemakers Studio. A collective facility and tasting room, the Studio was built by winemaker Eric Hamacher, and has become a major wine attraction.

Moving north up the AVA, we pass great vineyard after great vineyard, pretty much exclusively on the right arc of the horseshoe, including Lemelson's winery and its excellent Stermer Vineyard, and the Belle Pente estate. We catch Penner-Ash and its Dussin Vineyard on the right edge of the appellation, not far from the Shea Vineyard, made famous by winemakers like Lynn Penner-Ash and Ken Wright and many others with single-vineyard wines bearing the Shea name. Continuing north we encounter the cluster of small vineyards that make up the jewel-like Willa-Kenzie Estate, where Bernard and Ronni Lacroute created in a short time one of the standout wineries of Oregon. WillaKenzie's

The legendary 1975 Eyrie Vineyards South Block Pinot Noir, which won first place in the 1979 blind tasting in Paris against the finest Burgundy wines.

wines capture a lot of that "dark fruit and spice" that Ken Wright suggested come from these marine soils.

Some of the northernmost vineyards of the appellation, more isolated in the wooded hills between Yamhill and Gaston, belong to Elk Cove. Founded in 1974 as Oregon's eighth bonded winery, Elk Cove was the first vineyard in what is now this AVA. The lush dark fruit and sweet, but dense tannins of wines from the Roosevelt Vineyard, one of Elk Cove's most prized sites, offers a good example of what Pommard-clone wine from Yamhill-Carlton can taste like.

DUNDEE HILLS

TO DRIVE ON WORDEN HILL ROAD through the heart of the Dundee Hills, as I did with Lynn Penner-Ash, the winemaker who has worked vineyards of this AVA for over twenty years, is to pass as thickly through Oregon's wine history as we do vineyards. As we wound our way through the steep, gorgeous hills that swell up like giant, forceful bubbles from the valley floor, we were treated to beautiful views and some of Oregon's most famous locales, and practically each one has a story behind it for Penner-Ash. "There's Dick Erath's estate," she said after one turn on the road, and "There's David Lett's original planting," after another. We passed prestigious names like Domaine Serene, Archery Summit, Domaine Drouhin Oregon, Torii Mor, Cameron, Sokol Blosser. It's a who's-who of famous Oregon names.

This is unsurprising given that the famous Red Hills of Dundee are the most densely planted of all the AVAs and also the flower that blossomed around David Lett's first seed of a vineyard, planted in 1965. Also, in direct, almost vehement, contrast to its neighbor to the west, the Yamhill-Carlton District, Dundee's soils are famously volcanic in nature, with deep, iron-rich clay topsoils that offer the namesake color to the Red Hills.

When in the midst of the hills, the curvy roads can make orientation difficult. But there's no doubt as to where they end. Like the prow of ship cutting through the still valley floor, the magnificent Stoller Vineyards occupies the tapering, southernmost face of the hills. From the top of the vineyard we look can look out to the Coast Range to the west and the Eola Hills to the south, getting a sense of the way wind comes through the Van Duzer Corridor from the sea and heads up-valley, cooling the rest of the vineyards.

It is often said that the wines of the Dundee Hills are the most recognizable of all the Oregon AVAs. The same words keep coming up when people talk about them: red berry fruit, juicy, lush, fruit-forward and pretty. "It's not easy to isolate the various *terroirs* when you taste the wines of the Willamette Valley," Bill Stoller says. "But something about these Dundee Hills shows through. It was the first place to get planted and is usually the easiest wine to distinguish. Maybe there's a connection there."

MCMINNVILLE

WEST OF DUNDEE AND SOUTH OF CARLTON begins the McMinnville AVA. Nestled in the foothills of the Coast Range, the McMinnville AVA is fairly rugged territory, as the gentle Willamette Valley is consumed by brooding Pacific peaks. Because of its proximity to the Van Duzer Corridor, the low passage through the mountains, the McMinnville AVA receives early exposure to the marine air, keeping temperatures down. But it's also protected in the rain shadow, so rainfall there can be less than in some of the surrounding AVAs. Soils not only consist of marine sedimentary typically found in this area, but are also characterized by a unique occurrence of marine basalt.

Momtazi estate vineyard and natural reservoir overlooks Mt. Hood at sunrise, McMinnville, Oregon.

Vista Balloon tour over Eola Hills, Oregon

With only about 600 acres of the total 40,000 under vine, the area has yet to be really developed. The Hyland Vineyard, planted in the mid-1970s, is one of the most famous sites in the area, though the Momtazi Vineyard, with its 225 acres of biodynamically farmed vines, is rapidly gaining prestige among winemakers eager to purchase the fruit. Ken Wright has also made a wine from the Meredith Mitchell vineyard since 1988. Hotshot former Napa winemaker Robert Brittan arrived not long ago and under the label Brittan Vineyards has been seeing the first, highly encouraging vintages off of his own property near Momtazi. Interest in the region continues to grow.

Zenith Vineyard surrounding St. Innocent Winery, Eola Hills, Oregon.

EOLA-AMITY HILLS

THE SOUTHERNMOST OF THE SUB-AVAS, the Eola-Amity Hills region is a massive outcropping of basalt somewhat disconnected from the other winegrowing centers. But while the AVA may be slightly distant, it enjoys an outsized reputation for quality among wine producers, many of whom venture from other regions to source grapes here. The rep is in no small part thanks to the quality of wines issued by some of the AVA's more prominent producers, wineries like Cristom, Bethel Heights and St. Innocent. Several of the independent vineyards have also made names for themselves—Canary Hill, Carter, Seven Springs, Temperance Hill—in single-vineyard bottlings by outside producers.

While its soils are similar to what we find in the other discretely volcanic area, the Dundee Hills, the Eola Hills region is notable for some consistent distinctions in its wines. As Mark Vlossak of St. Innocent recalls, repeatedly in blind tastings against wines from the similar Dundee soils, the descriptors for Eola Hills were always distinct and consistent. "Each time, people described the wines here as darker, spicier, with coffee and chocolate overtones," he says, "a little more rustic tannin, a little more wild."

Such differences may arise from the fact that the Eola Hills lie just opposite the Van Duzer Corridor and are the first landmass to experience the rush of cold, marine air. This especially affects the exposed vineyards on the western side of the hills. Most of the vineyards in this region, however, are situated on the eastern slopes, looking across the valley at the Cascade Range.

AND BEYOND

WILLAMETTE VALLEY WINEGROWING DOESN'T END with the Eola Hills. Continuing south, the temperature gets warmer, but remains well within the ideal range for growing Pinot Noir. One only need taste the wines of Broadley or Benton-Lane to discern that.

In addition, a couple of the state's larger quality producers, King Estate and Willamette Valley Vineyards, are located down here. Though both wineries source grapes from all over the state, their "home" vineyards lie south of the sub-AVAs described above. King Estate is south of Eugene and makes a Pinot Noir from mountain vineyards there. Willamette Valley Vineyards' estate vineyards are just south of Salem on a pretty, sloping volcanic hillside topped with clay loam. It makes a lovely wine, flush with floral and spice notes.

Steve and Carol Girard, owners of Benton-Lane Winery, walk estate vineyards near Monroe (between Corvallis and Eugene), Oregon.

Steve Girard of Benton-Lane says that the northern end of the valley may be more popular largely because of its cluster of small towns and its proximity to Portland, the state's largest city. "We chose to be down here, though, because we think the soils are just the same, but the weather's a little bit better. It's warmer and the weather's more predictable." Over time, it's likely that others will take his point and venture down here. But today, it's still somewhat sleepy on the wine front.

CALIFORNIA

HIGH QUALITY PINOT NOIR IS MADE possible in California by one thing and one thing only: the world's greatest air conditioner, the Pacific Ocean. Far more reliable than an air conditioner in an old hotel and vastly more powerful than the systems used to cool Texas convention centers, the cooling of the Pacific operates consistently on schedule, keeping parts of the coast well ventilated with chilly blasts of wind and quickly rushing blankets of cool, damp fog. Its cycle is set to run on mornings and evenings, so the afternoons in most places are the hottest times.

What makes California Pinot Noir unique is that it is the product of a well-cooled hot place. With few exceptions, all top notch California Pinot grows in a strip within twenty-five miles of the sea. Most of the California coast is protected from the Pacific by a long range of coastal mountains. The west side of the mountains—the Pacific side—is too cold to ripen wine grapes unless the vineyard is high enough in the ridges to be above the fog line. The land east of the mountains cools when the fog and wind take advantage of natural gaps—river deltas, low-lying hills, or San Pablo Bay—to steal through. Without that penetration, California is a hot, sunny place that gets no summer rain. The heat is necessary to ripen the grapes, but what gives California Pinot much of its fruit-forward, juicy richness is the direct, unmediated interplay of extremes—extreme cool to extreme warmth, extreme fog to extreme sun.

ANDERSON VALLEY

MOST OF MENDOCINO COUNTY, LOCATED DIRECTLY north of Sonoma and Napa counties, is too hot to grow Pinot Noir, as its central valleys are well insulated from the sea by an intimidating series of wild, wooded mountains. But the Anderson Valley, a 20-mile-long, needle-thin slash in the mountains following the Navarro River, is perfectly situated to receive just enough fog and cold to make some of the freshest, most vibrant Pinot Noir in California.

Between valley and sea is a nine-mile-long forest

Edmeades vineyard in the Anderson Valley.

Kendall-Jackson's Annapolis Vineyard, Sonoma Coast.

Pacific fog rolls in to cool high vineyards on the Sonoma Coast.

of redwoods. From the last of the big trees, the valley ascends in a northwest-to-southeast direction. The fog and cool air slow their march as the valley runs inland. Thus the vineyards in the area of the northernmost town, Navarro, have the coolest weather. Temperatures gradually rise around the town of Philo and get warmer still at Boonville, the valley's hub. Soils are mainly composed of clay loams and alluvial gravel deposits on the valley floor, while thin loams over sandstone cover the hills. The valley has shown the ability to make complex and balanced Pinot Noirs not too high in alcohol.

Because of its remoteness (three hours minimum from San Francisco), Anderson Valley's vineyard development has been slow. Its first Pinot producers—Navarro, Husch and Lazy Creek Vineyards—planted Pinot Noir in the early 1970s and mostly had the valley to themselves until others started coming in the 1980s. The most important addition was the Champagne house

of Louis Roederer, arriving in 1982 to found its Roederer Estate winery, still one of the most respected sparkling wine producers in California. Roederer brought attention, resources and legitimacy, and helped to put Anderson Valley on the map. The next twenty years saw the gradual but accelerating development of the region's valley floor and hillsides. While some larger operations have made their mark—Goldeneye (founded by the Napa giant Duckhorn winery) for one, and Kendall-Jackson, which farms large plantings on the hillsides—the Anderson Valley has largely been a story of small producers.

High-end boutique producers like Williams Selyem and Littorai brought the media spotlight in the 1990s with high-scoring and hard-to-get Pinots. Another small producer, Wells Guthrie of Copain, has since made the region his own, becoming the single-vineyard king of the Anderson Valley with individually

bottled Pinots from various locales. In addition, fine new small producers like Black Kite, Macphail and Breggo have all garnered recent acclaim. High in the hills Demuth Winery has contributed its name to highly prized bottlings by such emerging wine labels as Anthill Farms, Adrian Fog and Skewis, while making a very nice wine of its own.

Lack of available land and remoteness will keep Anderson Valley small, but its esteem among Pinot lovers who love its refined style will continue to grow.

Anderson Valley, Mendocino County.

SONOMA COAST

THE OFFICIAL SONOMA COAST AVA, which encompasses 500,000 acres and includes other AVAs like the Sonoma Valley and Russian River, is such a joke that most people don't speak of it with regard to its official capacity. Rather, they talk about the "true" Sonoma Coast, the thin band of coastal ridges stretching from Bodega Bay up to the town of Gualala, near the Sonoma-Mendocino county line. With its wild, tree-covered peaks poking out above the invasion of sea fog, the true Sonoma Coast is one of the most visually dramatic wine regions in North America.

The Sonoma Coast started to emerge relatively recently with the ascent of the Hirsch Vineyard in the late '80s and early '90s. At the time, Pinot Noir was just coming into fashion and those star-making boutique wineries—Williams Selyem, Littorai, and

Kistler, to name a few—recognized the exceptional fruit and started bottling a Hirsch-designated Pinot Noir. Soon the area was awash in high-end Pinot. Flowers Vineyard & Winery's Pinot became a hot item, and Helen Turley's Marcassin Vineyards wines brought the rare aura of "cult Pinot" to the region. In the meantime, other notable projects were getting started. South African couple Linda and Lester Schwartz began planting their Fort Ross Vineyards in 1994. Brothers Nick and Andy Peay started planting the Peay Vineyards in 1997.

The two major factors influencing climate on the Sonoma Coast are proximity to the ocean and vineyard elevation. Just because a vineyard is close to the ocean doesn't mean it's going to experience the coolest temperatures. Proximity to the ocean can be mitigated if vineyards are located above the fog line, just as vineyards farther from the ocean's chill can be warmer if they're set at a lower altitude.

As Andy Peay sees it, there are three unofficial sections of the Sonoma Coast: "In the southern and northern sections of coast, where we are, the vineyards are planted at lower altitudes. We're at about 800 feet, meaning we get bathed in fog every morning and evening." In the central section, vineyards like Hirsch or Fort Ross—which are only a mile from the sea—occupy higher ground between 1,200–1,700 feet and actually harvest earlier in the season and make riper-tasting wines.

Close proximity to the sea does present a vulnerability to wind and weather, though, which are dangerous particularly from late spring to early summer during a vine's bud break and flowering stages. Bad weather at this time can destroy infant clusters. The true Sonoma Coast can receive from 80 to 120 inches of rain each year, but virtually none during the summer months of the vine's ripening season.

"We are perhaps the Russian Roulette experts," says Linda Schwartz of Fort Ross. "We're doing everything that's counterintuitive. We're on hills that are too steep, too close to the water. But we would rather be unsafe than make uninteresting wine." Sometimes they come close to losing in Russian Roulette, as in 2005, when bad weather caused them only to reap 25% of a normal harvest. But most often they win, in the best years making wines that Schwartz says "have the lusciousness of the Russian River and the structure of the Anderson Valley."

When thinking of Sonoma Coast Pinot Noir, think of intensity of fruit flavor, supported by a delicate earthiness and a bright acid structure. Wines like

Green Valley, California.

Failla's Sonoma Coast, Occidental, and Hirsch bottlings, display these qualities to a tee. "It's possible to make full-flavored, ripe and naturally complex Pinot here at lower alcohol levels," Ehren Jordan of Failla says. "That's one reason I love it—the wines just taste better with that more modest form."

RUSSIAN RIVER VALLEY

WHEN VISITORS TO SAN FRANCISCO ASK ME which wine region they should visit, I always recommend the Russian River. Few regions better exemplify the lyrical beauty of California, as redwood groves and vineyards alternate in a chessboard pattern across the landscape. One of the cradles of modern Pinot Noir in California, it is an easy day trip from the city.

With more than 10,000 acres of vineyard land, the Russian River Valley is a large, diverse and somewhat undefined appellation. Unlike, say, the Anderson Valley, it doesn't have an easily described shape. "I can relate to why it's hard to get your mind around it," Randy Ullom, wine master for Kendall-Jackson, told me. "If they were going to redo the appellation, they would certainly split it up many times over, because you've got the upper reaches, the middle reaches, the lower reaches, the south end pushing toward Rohnert Park, the Petulama Gap, right on the coast, and over valley and hill. It's diverse, all right."

The coolest part is in the southwestern section, which encompasses the smaller Green Valley AVA. Hartford Court, Marimar Torres, Freeman and Iron Horse all make Pinot Noir in the Green Valley. One of the most important vineyards, Keefer Ranch is there. Its fruit has become famous for the exceedingly well balanced, elegant wines producers like Failla, Patz & Hall, and Tandem are making. The unique Goldridge soil—a sandy, well-draining loam low in nutrients —in this area can imbue wines with discernible minerality.

To the north and west of Green Valley lies the heart of the region. Scenic Westside Road is a Pinot Noir hall-of-fame promenade with Gary Farrell, Williams Selyem and Rochioli wineries, makers of some of the most iconic and definitive Russian River Pinots. And while this is hallowed ground, it doesn't mean that there isn't room for new producers. The McWilliams family, formerly of Texarkana, managed to purchase land immediately in between Williams Selyem and Rochioli for their Pinot winery, Arista. Mark McWilliams, a relative newcomer to the area, marvels at the almost mechanical consistency of the climate. "It's like clockwork here and very reliable," he says. "As we get into July and August you get this amazing cooling effect from the fog—a quiet and a peace that you can feel with that damp, cool air. You can almost taste that cool climate in the grapes. The fog comes in at night. It's so thick in the mornings that we can't even see the tasting room from the house, and it's only a few hundred feet. The fog burns off around mid-day and then it suddenly warms up to 85, 90 degrees for a few hours in the afternoon." The result is sappy and lush Pinot Noir, rich in fruit flavors.

Due east of Green Valley is the area around Lynmar Winery, a microclimate governed by the Santa Rosa wetlands. "Without this, one of the largest freshwater wetlands in the state" says Lynmar's winemaker Hugh Chapelle, "the area would be a much warmer place, maybe too warm for high quality Pinot. By evaporative cooling, it provides a cooler and more consistent temperature." Lynmar's Quail Ridge Hill Vineyard Pinot is repeatedly one of the finest Pinot Noirs in the state.

Northeast of this area is Olivet Lane, the home

Domaine Alfred vineyards in Edna Valley.

Talley vineyards, Arroyo Grande, Central Coast, California.

"If you need to coax the very best out of a living thing, turning it into a unique reflection of its origin, then I think you might want the nurturing, patient, intuitive qualities women seem to have in great supply."

—MILLA HANDLEY, HANDLEY CELLARS

View toward Williams Selyem from Arista's vineyards in the Russian River.

of DeLoach, and to the north, Sonoma Cutrer and La Crema wineries. This is one of the Russian River Valley's warmer areas, where on a summer day the temperature can be 10 degrees higher than the Green Valley. Good Pinot can be made here, but DeLoach's excellent single-vineyard Pinots (made by the famous Greg La Follette) come mostly from the Green Valley and the Sonoma Coast.

CARNEROS

IF THE RUSSIAN RIVER VALLEY makes an impression with its forests and stands of redwoods, much of Carneros, with its dune-like hills covered completely in vines, is just as notable for its lack of such things. The invocation of dunes is not totally inapt, as Carneros is practically seaside. It's the ti-ara atop of the head San Pablo Bay, the vast inland incursion of Pacific seawater that comes in through the Golden Gate. Its

A ZD Pinot Noir was the first wine to recognize the Carneros region on a label.

rich clays and silty loams are what's left from the receding of the bay over thousands of years.

Carneros is also the rare AVA that crosses two counties—in this case, rivals Napa and Sonoma. As a part of both counties, Carneros has long been farmed for grapes, though it wasn't until the 1960s and '70s that Pinot really took off here. Without the cooling morning fog and consistent afternoon breeze off San Francisco Bay, Carneros can be a very warm place indeed (it's at the same latitude as Sicily). The heat becomes apparent summer days around noon, as the sun mercilessly beats down and there's nary a tree in sight for shade. But like clockwork the cool sea breeze

starts up just after lunch and Carneros becomes its cool, windblown self again.

Francis Mahoney's Carneros Creek Winery, founded in 1972, is given much of the credit for igniting Pinot production in this area, but there was Pinot here long before that, going back to the 1940s and the Stanly Ranch. The modern era effectively kicked off in 1969 when Norman deLeuze and Gino Zepponi bought grapes and made Carneros Pinot Noir under their fledgling wine label, ZD, which today is one of the oldest continuous producers of Carneros Pinot Noir. Brett deLeuze, Norman's son, remembered the style of that wine. "It was what I consider traditional Pinot Noir," he told me, "a well-balanced wine, good acidity, cherry type flavors. It's a lighter red in both color and texture. Very classical, and that's what Carneros can offer." It's those qualities which no doubt encouraged Dick Ward and David Graves to found Saintsbury in 1981, and led a number of European-based sparkling wine houses to set up shop in the area, notably Spain's cava giants Freixenet and Codorniu (with Gloria Ferrer and Codorniu Napa, now Artesa) and Champagne's Taittinger, Mumm, and Moët et Chandon (with Domaine Carneros, Mumm Napa and Domaine Chandon, respectively).

But, according to deLeuze, ZD's Pinots—and Carneros'—have changed over time. "With the development of the Dijon clones and viticultural advances in canopy management and irrigation, we've been able to achieve wines in a more modern style that are deeper and darker," he said. "I think, actually, our wines are better than they've ever been."

Darker, yet balanced and elegant Pinots are found

throughout Carneros these days. Highly respected producers like Etude and Sinskey continue to garner acclaim for their excellent wines. Newer projects like the Donum Estate make lovely wine, while famous vineyard names like Hyde, Hudson and Sangiacomo find their way onto dozens of bottles from some of the most talented boutique producers.

CENTRAL COAST

PINOT-CULTURE PERSISTS DOWN THE COAST from San Francisco. Just south of the city begins the Santa

Vineyards at Vine Hill Winery, Santa Cruz Mountains, California.

Cruz Mountains region, where Pinot history is traced back to a character named Martin Ray, who planted a steep hilltop in the 1930s and '40s near the town of Saratoga. Ray's venture ultimately became what is now Mount Eden Vineyards, which still produces high quality Pinot Noir from the striking mountain site, with its panoramic view of Silicon Valley. In the 1970s, David Bruce got started, making a name for Pinot Noir with his eponymous winery at a time when Pinot wasn't well known. Because of its proximity to Silicon Valley, its sheer hillsides and environmental constraints on land usage, the Santa Cruz Mountains AVA will never become a huge producer. Today, only about 180 acres are devoted to Pinot Noir. But it tends to be of very good quality, making high acid, earthy, lively wines. Brothers Jim and Bob Varner have been making lovely, lean Pinots for decades, while newcomers like Rhys and Windy Oaks are attracting buzz from connoisseurs.

Continuing down Highway 101 brings us through the Salinas Valley, where field after field grows enough broccoli, asparagus and lettuce to feed the nation. Green vegetables are not pleasantly associated with wine, though, which is why vineyards are planted high above the valley on a narrow, steep bench designated as the Santa Lucia Highlands AVA. Separating the highlands from coastal towns like Monterey and Carmel is the Santa Lucia Range. The name most associated with the area is Gary Pisoni, a vegetable farmer turned wine celebrity (thanks to his wild-man, never-met-a-party-he-didn't-like persona), who was the first major advocate of Pinot. His hillside property is peppered with several discreet Pinot vineyards, whose fruit is sold to many of the state's hottest brands—Siduri, Patz & Hall, Arcadian, and Peter Michael among them—which have in turn made Pisoni famous. (With his sons, Mark and Jeff, Pisoni also makes a lovely wine under his the family name.) The vineyards closest to the valley's open northern end (where cold sea air enters) are the coolest. Temperatures rise as the valley plunges south. Wines from here are known more for lushness and intensity, rather than delicacy, and show a preponderance of rich, juicy fruit.

SOUTH CENTRAL COAST

PINOT'S FINAL STRETCH DOWN THE CALIFORNIA COAST starts just south of the town of San Luis Obispo, where the Edna Valley and Arroyo Grande valleys find themselves nestled in the hills. Both are small appellations with steadily rising reputations for Pinot Noir. The Edna Valley is the bigger of the two appellations and has largely been recognized for its Chardonnay. Good Pinot Noir can be made here, though, as demonstrated by wineries like Baileyana, Wedell, Domaine Alfred and Stephen Ross. A component of limestone in the soils makes somewhat mineral wines with fine-boned structures. Arroyo Grande is known primarily for Talley Vineyards, owned by highly respected farmers who bottle their own wine and sell some as vineyard designates to other top producers.

Far more famous to Pinot lovers are the next two AVAs: the Santa Maria Valley and below it, the Sta. Rita Hills (pronounced Santa Rita, but they were kept from using the exact name because of a pre-existing

region in Chile). Both AVAs take advantage of what is a singular occurrence of the coastline's architecture: the intrusion in the vertical orientation of California's coast range with an oddity, a transverse range running east-west. This interruption amounts to a big gash in the dyke holding back all that cold sea air, which, naturally, rushes in fiercely. Essentially just one great big open plain, the Santa Maria Valley is unprotected, so most of the vineyards tend to cower away from the ocean fury to the tune of about 18 miles and take shelter in some creases along the back hills of the valley.

Tucked in those creases is the Bien Nacido Vineyard, first planted in the late 1960s. Perhaps the most famous Pinot vineyard in California, Bien Nacido's grapes are made into vineyard-designated

Acacia vineyards in Los Carneros.

Pinots by dozens of top producers. Foremost among them is Jim Clendenen of Au Bon Climat, who has perhaps done more than anyone to put California Pinot Noir on the map. He's accomplished this by relentlessly traveling the world with his encyclopedic knowledge of winemaking, rapid-fire rhetorical style, strong opinions and long, blond Viking locks. A relentless railer against overripe, high alcohol, fruit-bomb Pinots, Clendenen backs up his rhetoric with great wine (from many vineyards, including Bien Nacido and his own Santa Maria property, Le Bon Climat). Other top producers whose Pinots bear the Bien Nacido stamp include Hartley-Ostini, Lane Tanner, Tantara, Foxen and Ambullneo.

The soils of Santa Maria are fairly consistent sandy loams. The wines are much prettier than the flat, dull scenery, tending toward smooth textures with medium-to-light tannins and a pleasant earthiness. Thanks to the cool weather, acidity is bright.

There is more to Santa Maria than Bien Nacido. Foxen Vineyards has developed a sterling reputation, and Costa d'Oro—made by Au Bon Climat alum Gary Burk—always seems a definitive example of Santa Maria fruit: strawberry and cherry flavors, with an earthy note and a dash of spice. Notably, Jess Jackson (of Kendall-Jackson) and his wife Barbara Banke bought a huge tract of vineyard in 1986, and called the wine Cambria. Its Julia's Vineyard bottling is typically a standout.

About 25 miles south of Santa Maria lies the Sta. Rita Hills AVA, which in the last few years has garnered much attention. A collection of low lying hills

that crop up just east of the town of Lompoc, where the valley opens up again to the ocean, the Sta. Rita Hills region is just as cold as the Santa Maria Valley. What primarily differentiates one from the other are Sta. Rita's hills—which break the wind—and its more diverse soils. These include clay loams, Monterey shale, sandy loams and gravels with a high content of calcareous matter, whereas the Santa Maria soils are mostly sands and loams.

The region was basically founded for Pinot Noir in 1971 when Richard Sanford and Michael Benedict planted their Sanford and Benedict vineyard, which almost immediately started producing jaw-dropping wines. "I'll always remember when in 1976," Richard Sanford remembered fondly, "a prominent wine critic came and called our wines 'a *grand cru* from a Lompoc barn.'" Until the early 1980s, Sanford was pretty much alone in the region with one other producer, Lafond (who planted at around the same time but didn't make as much of a name), and later Babcock. Vineyard developers tended to head to the flatter, more easily planted, sure bet of Santa Maria rather than take on the lesser-known Sta. Rita Hills. In the mid-'90s, the region finally exploded, as a series of highly regarded wines

issued forth from very young brands like Melville, Fiddlehead, Brewer-Clifton, Foley, Clos Pepe and Sea Smoke. Richard Sanford, thanks to a series of business deals gone awry, lost and regained his winery and then lost it again. But he persisted through the turmoil and his new label, Alma Rosa, makes use of personal vineyards he planted in the 1980s.

The Sea Smoke vineyard in particular, with its glorious southern hillside exposures, has become somewhat emblematic of the region, not least for its magnificent appearance, but also for the dark, rich, voluptuous nature of its wines. Victor Gallegos, Sea Smoke's general manager and a trained enologist explains the wines: "Our style is unapologetically New World. I love Burgundy, but that's not we make here. Remember, Sta. Rita Hills *terroir* starts with latitude, which is the same as Tunisia. We may be as cool as any region on the West Coast, but the intensity of the sun here is serious. We work with our site, rather than against it." Which isn't to say that other sites don't yield other styles. Jim Clendenen has long made a lighter, more elegant wine from the Sanford and Benedict Vineyard, and Richard Sanford continues to make such a wine at Alma Rosa. Some wines—like those from Foley or

Clos Pepe—are in between Sea Smoke and Alma Rosa in style. Brewer-Clifton, one of the first "cult" Pinots, is Old World in style, but New World in its size and fruit intensity.

In fact, the mixtures of stylistic differences in the Sta. Rita Hills serve to remind us how young California Pinot Noir really is. Winemakers get only one vintage a year, so change is slow. But as time decides what styles work the best for this and all regions, winemakers will adjust.

Fall color in Los Carneros.

ODDS AND ENDS

IT SEEMS CRAZY TO MENTION THREE of the country's most important and historic Pinot Noir wines under the heading "odds and ends," but Hanzell, Calera and Chalone don't fit neatly into any of California's major Pinot AVAs. Calera and Chalone, both in the Central Coast region, have their own AVAs.

Calera is the sole occupant of Mount Harlan, its AVA. Founded by Josh Jensen in the early 1970s, Calera is the story of one man's obsessive quest to find limestone soils suitable for Pinot Noir. He found them, but it took him to a remote mountaintop in San Benito County, 25 miles from the sea, in the middle of wine nowhere.

In terms of nowhere-ness, the Chalone AVA is Mount Harlan's equal, if not better. Located across the valley from the Santa Lucia Highlands, miles into a desert of barren rock and scrub at 1,800 feet of elevation, the area was first planted in the 1890s. Perhaps the draw was—as for Jensen—limestone, which the site has in abundance. Chalone's Pinot Noir started to make a name for itself in the 1950s, and in the 1960s a brand was born with the Chalone name. The wines can be very interesting, if sometimes a little baked from the high heat of the site and the lack of ground moisture. In addition to the brand called Chalone, there are other producers making wine from the AVA, including Michaud and Testarossa.

Finally, back up in Sonoma, there's a little winery called Hanzell. Nestled in hills overlooking the Sonoma Valley and town of Sonoma, Hanzell exists in a bit of a vortex, since the largest concentration of Pinot in Sonoma is either south in Carneros or west in the Russian River Valley. But Hanzell, founded in 1956, is one of the first wineries in California to be specifically devoted to Burgundian varieties, and

has improbably made beautiful Pinot Noir wines that have stood the test of time. Though ownership has changed hands several times, Hanzell's track record has not suffered. The winery is better known for Chardonnay than Pinot, but Hanzell's Pinot Noir evolved in the last few years under the stewardship of Hanzell's former winemaker, Michael Terrien. Made from old vines, old clones and (until recently) fairly old methods, the wines are known for amazing savory complexity and an ability to, well, get better and better until they're very old.

Sea Smoke estate vineyard overlooking Santa Ynez river, Sta. Rita Hills, Central Coast, California.

Sea Smoke Cellars vineyards in the Sta. Rita Hills.

"Only when someone has taken the time to truly understand its potential can pinot be coaxed into its fullest expression. And when that happens, its flavors are the most haunting and brilliant and subtle and thrilling and ancient on the planet"

—MILES IN SIDEWAYS

Evening fog rolls over the Foley vineyards in the Sta. Rita Hills.

Allen Holstein, vineyard manager, Dundee Hills, Oregon.

Joe Rochioli, grower, Russian River, Sonoma.

Roger Vlasik, grower, Mistletoe Vineyards, Dallas, Oregon.

Ulisses Valdez, vineyard manager, Russian River, Sonoma.

Charles Bacigalupi, grower, Russian River, Sonoma.

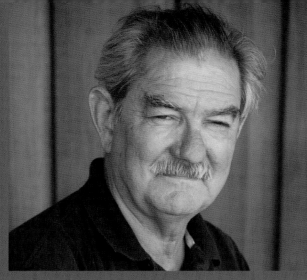

Larry Hyde, grower, Hyde Vineyards, Carneros, Napa County.

Gary Pisoni, grower, Pisoni Vineyards, Santa Lucia Highlands.

Dan and Helen Dishay, growers, Freedom Hill Vineyard near Salem, Oregon.

Joel Meyer, vineyard manager, Dundee Hills, Oregon.

Wes and Chandra Hagen, growers, Clos Pepe, Sta. Rita Hills.

Marcy Keefer, grower, Keefer Ranch, Green Valley, Sonoma.

Ken Wright holds a sample of the sandstone dirt from his Abbott Claim vineyard, where soil depths reach to 30 inches before mother rock, Yamhill-Carlton, Oregon.

"Pinot is more sensitive to almost every decision because it's such a transparent variety. It reflects almost everything you do."

—HUGH CHAPELLE, LYNMAR

Snow covers Adelsheim's Calkin's Lane estate vineyard and irrigation pond, Oregon.

A YEAR IN THE VINEYARD

THE CHARACTER AND HANDLING of the vineyard is the key to any good wine, and this is especially true in the case of Pinot Noir. Being more sensitive than most grapes to the slightest alterations in temperature, moisture and light, Pinot requires its viticulturists to be not only hard-working and skillful, but also extremely clever.

A full year of life in the vineyard is not so different from a year of life in a human. It's marked by seasonal change and the accompanying shifts in behavior and mood. As are our lives, the vine's year is stamped with significant days and periods. Though grapevines don't celebrate birthdays and national holidays, they do experience momentous occasions such as bud break, flowering and veraison.

While tending a vineyard requires a fundamental annual routine, there's no set formula as to how and exactly when each move must occur. A vintner has significant room for creativity and individual style when it comes to planning and planting a vineyard, shaping its vines and tending its soils. These factors, though rarely described in mainstream wine discussions, can

Winter snow over dormant Pinot Noir vine in Oregon.

Make no mistake, the stakes are high. Poor players can leave the vineyard empty handed or with wine of marginal quality. Good players cash in their chips in the form of delicious Pinot Noir year in and year out. With that in mind, let's take a look at a game of "Pinot poker" from the first hand and watch how the game progresses. Ante up, players. The tight-lipped, absolutely inscrutable Mother Nature is set to deal the cards.

WINTER

VINEYARDS ARE RARELY more beautiful than at the end of harvest, when for a couple of weeks their leaves, marching in nature's autumn parade, turn luminous shades of gold and red before bidding adieu. It's a festive and heartening display, at once a spirited commemoration of a job well done and a sentimental farewell for another six months.

While this moment might appear to be the end of the season and time for a well-earned Maui vacation, nothing could be further from the truth. There's much work to be done in the winter, which marks not only the end of the current year, but equally so the beginning of the new year for the vine.

Most importantly, winter work consists of pruning. Pruning a vine is more complicated than getting out a pair of hedge shears and snip-snipping at a wall of shrubbery. Winter pruning has massive impact on the way the vine grows and the quality of fruit it will ultimately produce. As Tony Soter of Oregon's Soter Vineyards told me, "It's the part of winegrowing that no one really sees and that most people don't really understand. And while there's definitely a science to pruning, there's also an art to it that comes from understanding the nature of the Pinot vine and the soils and climate in which it grows."

have significant impact on the taste of Pinot in the glass. As one winemaker, Adam Lee of Siduri, who makes Pinot Noir in both California and Oregon, put it to me, "Sometimes I think of tending a vineyard as a game of poker. You are dealt some cards, but every year they're different, and you don't ever play them the same way. When you put a card down, you have to wait and see what card the vine plays in response and base your next move on what it does. You have to read its intentions and know its habits. And this goes on and on."

Winter pruning is really a form of advance planning, mapping out the way the vine will grow in the coming year. The goal is to encourage the vine to produce healthy bunches of grapes, in the desired quantity that ripen evenly and in a timely manner.

All spring growth will occur from the buds left on the plant the previous winter. It's an obvious ratio: The more buds left, the more bunches of grapes there will be. The optimal number of bunches is entirely related to the vine's ability to ripen them. On the one hand, winegrowers want as much crop as possible, since this relates directly to their bank accounts. On the other hand, the fruit has to consist of small, ripe grapes, otherwise the quality of the resulting wine will suffer. An unmanaged vine will produce an overabundance of fruit to better its chances of spreading its seed and reproducing. The job of the viticulturist is to divert the vine's energy from producing more fruit than it can successfully ripen to producing just enough ripe fruit that will be irresistibly delicious. (Conventional wisdom has it that sweet, ripe grapes are the vine's evolutionary reproductive strategy to attract birds and thereby spread its seed. However, these same grapes have done a much bigger number on humans, who have given over millions of acres of the earth's surface to the humble vine and do much of its reproductive work for it.)

For quality-minded Pinot growers, who work mostly in cool climates where ripening is no piece of cake, the question is: How many buds to leave? Typically, the answer is the number of buds contained on only one or two canes.

The bony vines are left to stand through the cold winter months in a state of meditative dormancy. Then—often in cold, soggy weather—skilled vineyard workers don their scarves and fingerless gloves and head to the vineyard to remove the majority of last

Recently pruned Pinot Noir vines in snow at Rex Hill winery, Oregon.

year's canes. What they leave is precious, as these canes already possess this year's and next year's grapes, wine and good times. The good Pinot poker player must always think ahead, and winter pruning is the first hand.

WillaKenzie Estate vineyard manager Daniel Fey pulls canes off freshly pruned vines, Oregon.

Positioning trellis for Pinot Noir vines, Willamette Valley, Oregon.

Winter rains flood Rochioli's vineyards in Sonoma's Russian River appellation overlooked by Mount St. Helena in neighboring Napa County.

To preserve the life of the soil, hand hoeing is used for weed control under the vines rather than herbicides. WillaKenzie Estate, Oregon.

SPRING

WITH WINTER PRUNING COMPLETE, winegrowers can relax a little. Viticulturists will typically prepare the soil for the coming year, plowing to aerate it and animate it. As the weather changes, spring rains douse the countryside, grasses grow green and wildflowers decorate the hillsides. The Pinot Noir vine begins to stir.

As spring begins, a subtle change is noticeable on the vine's nubs. First, a little bump appears. Over a period of a couple of weeks, the bump swells a little each day, until finally, it breaks open and the little tip emerges—the birth of a shoot. It happens on every bud left from the previous year's pruning and signals— glory be!—the start of the new season. While this is cause to celebrate, revelry must be muted. Mother Nature, the dealer, still has in her possession many potentially disastrous cards.

Early rains freshen the dormant vineyards of Alma Rosa Winery in the Sta. Rita Hills.

All infants are vulnerable and the nascent shoot is no different. Caught between winter's dying gasps and summer's eager entrance, spring can be fraught with extreme and sometimes violent weather. To the vineyards, spring can bring heavy deluges, wind, cold weather and—most dangerous of all—frost.

"Pinot Noir is an early-budding variety," Lynn Penner-Ash of Oregon's Penner-Ash Wine Cellars told me, "so when it buds, you're still in a risky time for late season frost. The effect a major freeze can have on the little shoots can be devastating. The vineyard looks like it's been burned. You can lose a lot of crop." Therefore, growers plant Pinot vine-

yards in places where the risk of frost is as low as possible. This is one reason most Pinot is planted on slopes. Penner-Ash planted her estate Dussin Vineyard on slopes ranging in elevation from 350 to 500 feet above sea level. "Being heavier air," she added, "frost tends to fall into the valleys. Being on hillsides with some elevation often means that the vines can stay out of harm's way." This is not always the case. In 2008, California was struck by a rare spring frost and Pinot vineyards from sea level all the way up to 2,000 feet were damaged, some severely. There are ways to protect against frost. Some are as primitive as lighting fires in small stoves throughout the vineyard (seen mostly in Old World wine regions). More modern methods range from spraying water over the grapes to give them a (yes, counterintuitive) protective layer of ice to using helicopters with their whirling blades to dispatch the freezing air.

If the awakening Pinot vineyards avoid frost until the weather warms, the growth of the shoots can be remarkable, making visible progress on a daily basis. First tender, fuzzy leaves appear, sprouting like baby rabbit ears from the tiny shoot. Then the shoot extends its slender, tender length and more leaves emerge. Eventually little clusters of tiny spheres develop. While each cluster may look like a bunch of grapes—and this is what it will eventually become—it is actually an inflorescence, a group of unbloomed flowers.

The Pinot poker player during this time waits and hopes that the next card dealt by nature is a good one.

Pruning in Los Carneros, California.

SUMMER

SUMMER IS A GREAT SEASON for Pinot vineyards. What a pleasure it is to picnic near them, quaffing chilled bottles of last harvest's Pinot Noir rosé, just now reaching its juicy peak. Of course, crucial things are happening for the vine as well.

The two major occurrences for the Pinot vine are flowering and veraison. Flowering, which takes place anywhere from May to June depending on the warmth of the site and weather conditions, is an exceedingly sensitive time. During this time the inflorescence blooms and the vine self-pollinates. The result is what is called "fruit set." Pollen released by the flower's stamen drifts a very short distance to the ovary, creating the opportunity for grapes to be born. A good set provides the opportunity for a robust, healthy crop. "You sort of hold your breath during flowering," says Harry Peterson-Nedry of Oregon's Chehalem winery. "The inconsistencies of weather can play havoc with both the flowering vines and with the winemaker's sanity."

He says temperate, even and "well, boring" weather is best, while wind, rain, hail or cold can doom a fruit set. Poor fruit set is no indication of the quality of the wine, though, just the amount of crop. "Sometimes bad fruit set just means you won't have to do much crop thinning. Nature has selected the amount for you—and you can often end up with really high quality wine . . . just not much of it," Peterson-Nedry adds. Still, a good flowering and set is always preferable, the equivalent of being dealt face cards and aces. A great set gives the Pinot grower the chance to have a good-sized crop of high quality.

The little green bunches of grapes gather size and shape through the months of July and August. Over this time winegrowers inspect the vineyards and remove the weeds that would compete with the grapevines for precious groundwater. The vines are still in their vegetative growth period. As shoots continue to lengthen they will be trimmed accordingly and, climbing upward, they'll be trained along the wires of the trellis. The point is to keep the vine balanced, preserving enough leaves to absorb the right amount of sunlight to ripen the grapes, but not so many leaves as to suck the plant's energy into green growth. Leaves around the clusters may be removed in order to allow some sunlight onto the grapes, promoting color development. "Often you'll pull leaves on the eastern side of a vineyard row to expose the clusters to the morning sun," says Peterson-Nedry, "while keeping the leaves on the western side for protection against afternoon sun. The difference is that morning sun comes while the grapes are still cool,

Winter work at Melville Vineyards in California's Sta. Rita Hills includes burning the pruned canes and other vineyard debris.

while late afternoon sun can bake the grapes because the air's already so warm."

The grower likewise has a general idea about crop size at this time and may cut away some of the clusters of Pinot Noir to guarantee the better ripening of the others. This is known as "green harvest" and is a universally practiced measure for Pinot Noir. Without suitably low yields, a Pinot has very little chance at greatness.

The summer builds toward the final drama of the grapevine's year: veraison, the seven- to ten-day period in which the grapes change color from green to red. In Pinot poker, the winegrower's working on a straight and only needs one more card to take the pot.

AUTUMN

AS WE MOVE INTO SEPTEMBER, winegrowers are watching their grapes, as well as the skies, just about every day. Weather is key during this time because ripening is yet another precarious period. What kind of weather does Pinot Noir like to ripen in? "From veraison to harvest, if I could just have dry weather in between 72 and 79 degrees, that would be great," says Nick Peay of Peay Vineyards of the Sonoma Coast. "And of course a nighttime cold temperature to keep everything fresh."

The grower's hope is slow, steady ripening. Over these weeks, in the grapes several meters are

A vineyard worker applying environmentally friendly fungicides, including elemental sulphur, mineral oil and seaweed extracts. Revana Vineyard, Oregon.

"It seems if you push yourself to the extreme and manage your crop well, you are capable of truly exceptional wines. But then you won't be capable of having a tranquil life."

—LINDA SCHWARTZ, FORT ROSS VINEYARDS

Planting new Pinot Noir vines at Zenith Vineyards next to St. Innocent Winery, Eola Hills, Oregon.

Detail of planting a new Pinot Noir vine.

running, with the two most important being sugar accumulation and flavor development. What makes ripening tricky is that the meters move at their own independent paces. As Nick Peay says, "What I'm looking for is flavor ripeness, which is separate from sugar accumulation. It seems that the sugar accumulation is directly correlated to temperature. When you have lots of sunlight and lots of heat, there's a faster production of sugar. Flavor accumulation, on the other hand, doesn't seem to correlate with heat but with time. Cool sunlight therefore gives you the most chance to accumulate flavors before the sugar comes up." Heat-spikes during ripening, which may especially bedevil Pinot growers in California, can push sugars ahead of flavors. If the heat perists until harvest, it leads to the worst scenario: overly alcoholic, under ripe wines. However, achieving ripeness and sugar before the advent of autumn rain is traditionally more of a danger in Oregon than in California. Rain before harvest can lead to dilution of the juice or the growth of rot in the vineyard. Winegrowers become nervous addicts of Doppler weather radar. To carry on a conversation with growers during this period is often unfulfilling; their minds are on the vineyards.

But let's assume that the ripening period is ideal. The temperate days and cool nights have pushed harvest to mid- to late September. The vintners are out walking their vineyards every day, tasting grapes, testing acids and sugars, trying to determine levels of ripeness. If there's no sign of rain and the weather stays cool, vintners have the luxury of choosing their harvest time—that augurs a good vintage. Finally, the Pinot poker player lays his hand out on the table—the call to pick grapes is made.

No one making high quality Pinot Noir would even think to pick by machine, so hand-picking crews are assembled from all able bodies. They go through the vineyards row by row with their shears, gently dropping the red, succulent clusters into bins. The bins are collected and brought by truck to the winery for processing. The entire harvest can take anywhere from a week to several, depending on the weather. A lot of cold beer is consumed in the process, and attention transfers to the cellar.

"Sometimes I think of tending a vineyard as a game of poker. You are dealt some cards, but every year they're different, and you don't ever play them the same way."

—ADAM LEE, SIDURI

Bud break in Hanzell's Sessions Vineyard above the town of Sonoma.

Pinot Noir vine at inflorescence state, a group of unbloomed flowers.

New leaves, anointed with early morning dew, bring a promise of summer.

Pulling canes in Los Carneros, California.

How to Start a Pinot Noir Business

The one and only ingredient needed to produce wine is—quite obviously—grapes. Everything else, even bottles and corks, is negotiable (for instance, wine can be sold in kegs or sold in bulk). How a winemaker gets ahold of grapes is the larger question.

One needs land to grow the grapes, but not every wine producer owns land. So there are other models of grape procurement in the Pinot Noir industry, and each has its pros and cons.

ESTATE — This is the classic model in which the winery owns the land where the grapes are grown. Widely considered the most desirable format, even it has vulnerabilities.

PROS: Complete control over grape farming methods (vital to quality); marketing—customers love to visit and see the winemaking process; security—no one can take it away (as can sometimes happen with contracted fruit); consistency—farming the same land for years on end allows the winegrower to truly understand it and thus make better wine.

CONS: Inflexibility—the winemaker is locked into one source of grapes (in the case of catastrophic weather, the vineyard might be devastated, but other areas might be unaffected); cost—few can afford to buy, plant, farm and pay taxes on their own land.

CONTRACTING VINEYARD LAND — In this model the winemaker doesn't own the land but pays a fee per acre to the vineyard owner. The winemaker is in charge of all aspects of farming the land and shares the farming costs with the vineyard owner.

PROS: Control—the winemakers own pruning and irrigating regimes guide vine and grape growth; flexibility—the winemaker probably has several such contracts in place in different regions as a hedge against bad weather in one location.

CONS: Impermanence—because someone else owns the land, the winemaker is at risk of losing the vineyard (and its brand name, which customers might know), leading to gaps and inconsistencies; commitment—if a winemaker is going to pour such time and effort into farming someone else's property, why not just get a loan and purchase a property?

BUYING GRAPES — The opposite of the estate model. Grapes are either purchased by the ton or, increasingly, by the acre from growers who own the land and farm the vineyards themselves. By-the-acre contracts usually involve some agreement that the landowners will farm the vineyard to the winemakers' specifications.

PROS: Flexibility—winemakers can shop around for the best deals; cost—it can be more affordable and less capital-intensive to buy grapes than to grow them; time—winemakers can devote more effort to marketing their wine without having to worry about plowing and pruning.

CONS: Inconsistency—grape sources may change from year to year, leading to fluctuations in wine character; lack of control—without controlling the farming, it's impossible to guarantee quality.

NEGOCIANT — Finished wine is purchased from either the bulk market or directly from wineries. Then it's blended, repackaged and sold under a different brand name.

PROS: Efficiency—bulk wine is cheaper, and a skilled winemaker can blend disparate lots to make a better wine and sell it at significant profit; flexibility—the winemaker is free to hop around to find the best deals.

CONS: Feast or famine—in tough vintages there may be very little decent wine on the bulk market, while in good vintages there will be; low end—the negociant is a model for inexpensive or bargain wine and, with few exceptions, is not used to create high-end product.

Natural spring-fed reservoir at Momtazi Vineyard, McMinnville, Oregon.

Grow tubes protect young Pinot Noir vines.

Tualatin Estate Vineyards, Yamhill-Carlton, Oregon.

Clover ground cover at Elk Cove's estate vineyard, Yamhill-Carlton, Oregon.

Wildflower ground cover at Stoller vineyard, Dundee Hills, Oregon.

Early morning fog over vineyards in the northern Willamette Valley signal onset of fall and upcoming harvest.

What Is Ripe?

One of the most challenging questions facing Pinot Noir producers every harvest is when to pick. The easy answer is, of course, "When the grapes are ripe." If only it could be that simple. It turns out, however, that what constitutes ripeness is a subjective assessment: Do you like your bananas on the green side or well on the way to black? Sometimes weather conditions make harvesting decisions easy—it's about to rain!—but when it's warm and dry, as it often is in California and Oregon, winemakers may have the luxury of giving the grapes "hang time," and can make their own decisions about when to pick.

Hang time has, however, become a bit of a controversial term, as winemakers and critics argue about what constitutes acceptable styles of Pinot Noir. Some people say that hang time is just an excuse to let flavors become over ripe and the wine to become outsized and overly alcoholic, a style rewarded by some critics. Those who practice this style say that size and alcohol are natural effects of the Pacific climate and that neither matters if the wine tastes balanced.

"Hang time to allow a grape vine to come into balance is one thing," Jim Clendenen, of California's Au Bon Climat Winery, once told me.

Veraison.

Freshly harvested cluster of Pinot from

"Letting the grapes hang to achieve riper flavor is a stylistic choice." A passionate crusader against high alcohol and stewed flavors, Clendenen asks if more flavor is necessarily *better* flavor. "It's the question of whether you like fresh, just picked raspberries or stewed, cooked raspberry coulis and raspberry candy. What you're tasting in those Pinots is simply more sweetness and less acidity. Those wines don't go well with food and they don't age."

Brian Loring, who tends to make a riper and higher-in-alcohol style of Pinot Noir than Clendenen, writes in a blog on the website of *Wine Spectator* that he prefers to "wait for the flavors to develop… we rarely worry about sugar numbers." If the sugars get too high before achieving the flavors he likes, Loring says that "We can always add water to lower the sugar level (and resulting alcohol level) or add acid." He reflects on where our standard of Pinot Noir ripeness even comes from. "The vines don't care… [and] People have placed artificial rules and ideas on winemaking based on regional limits and personal preferences… So what is ripe?" he asks. "In my opinion, it's whatever a winemaker decides. What you, the consumer, need to decide is which winemaker you agree with."

Adam Campbell, winemaker at Elk Cove Vineyards, Oregon, checks grape ripeness to determine his harvest schedule.

Harvesting Pinot Noir.

Ken Wright with Savoya Vineyard managers Mark Gould and Seth Miller, at estate vineyard during harvest, Yamhill-Carlton, Oregon.

Pinot harvest in Los Carneros.

Harvesting Pinot Noir at Ayoub Vineyard, Dundee Hills, Oregon.

Harvesting Pinot Noir at Lemelson's Washer Vineyard, Oregon.

Vineyard crew at Goldeneye in the Anderson Valley.

Sustainability

One of the most powerful trends sweeping through the Pinot industry in the last decade has been the increasing commitment to sustainable farming. Oregon has made this a pillar of its grape growing industry, while a similar movement has taken hold throughout California.

"Sustainable" generally means farming vineyards using practices that allow the ecosystem to sustain itself without synthetic inputs. The University of California at Davis' wine program and others define "sustainable" in terms of the "three E's": environmental health, economic profitability and social and economic equity. Under the umbrella of sustainability are several specific methods of certified farming—such as biodynamic, organic, Low Input Viticulture and Enology (LIVE) and others—that guarantee its practitioners are using the approved methods they claim.

Organic viticulture takes sustainability a step further, referring to practices that focus on the entire natural ecosystem of winegrowing, including the plants and animals that inhabit that sphere. Biodynamic, which combines the terms "biologically dynamic," takes the organic notion one step further and considers the farm as a living organism unto itself that doesn't rely on external sources of inputs. In addition, biodynamism incorporates a spiritual and cosmic approach that aligns certain tasks with phases of the moon and planets.

Rob Sinskey of Robert Sinskey Vineyards, one of the most dedicated organic and biodynamic farmers in the Napa Valley and producer of excellent Pinot Noir from Carneros, offers an example of how it works and the depth of commitment required. "Successful organic farming doesn't happen overnight and involves finding the interrelationships that you can only understand over time. It took ten years before we were confident, and we made mistakes early on. After year two or three we had some amazing broadleaf weed issues and all kinds of things running amok. The vineyard looked like hell. We realized

Aerial view of rooftop solar panels at Stoller, the first Gold LEED Certified (Leadership in Energy and Environmental Design) winery in the United States.

that we had to keep forging ahead on the holistic level. We started to think about how and why weeds grow and how they are successful at destroying their competition. We can now use the weed's own abilities to clear the land, and then with correct timing, we can plant cover crops to smother the weeds out and thus add nutrients back to the soil. Then once we get a handle on the cover crops, we can bring in the sheep to graze the cover crop, keeping it under control. Now we're experimenting with chickens, too. You can see that the vineyard ecosystem just keeps growing."

Beyond the vineyards, though, are even more opportunities for sustainable practices. Witness Wil-lamette Valley Vineyards, one of the largest producers of Oregon Pinot. WVV offers recycling refunds for bottles and shipping materials returned to its tasting rooms. It runs its equipment and delivery trucks on biodiesel fuel, and even makes the fuel available to its employees. Likewise, taking this expansive view of sustainability leads to programs like Salud, Oregon's partnership between wineries and healthcare professionals to provide medical services to seasonal vine-yard workers and their families. In California, Talley Vineyards established The Fund for Vineyard and Farm Workers to provide everything from medical to legal assistance to these workers.

Just as researchers have discov-ered that drinking wine can be a healthy practice in life, winemak-ers are finding ways that growing it can be a healthy practice for the planet. But the final question one always wants to ask is: Do these practices lead to better-tasting wine? And, if so, which ones? We may soon have some answers. The Four Graces, a Willamette Valley winery, has planted a new vineyard on the face of a large hillside. One 25-acre block has been devoted to sustainable farming, and right next to it an equal sized and practically identical block will be farmed bio-dynamically. In a few years, when the vines are bearing fruit, any dif-ferences should become apparent.

Herbal tea of stinging nettle, dandelion and chamomile being dynamized in a flow form tower before being applied as a foliar spray at Momtazi Vineyard, McMinnville, Oregon.

Biodynamic preparations at Beaux Fréres, Ribbon Ridge, Oregon.

Clos Pepe's vineyards are at their most picturesque at the end of harvest when the vines turn golden. This is a contract vineyard and the grapes have already left for wineries such as Siduri and Loring who produce a single-vineyard "Clos Pepe" Pinot Noir.

On Clones

Discussion with almost any Pinot maker will before long descend to digitization. Numbers will begin to take over for words—667, 777, 113, 115, 420A, 5C. These are the decidedly unromantic names of some of the various clones and rootstocks that have come to populate the Pinot vineyards of the West Coast. (To be fair, some clones have actual names: for instance, Swan, Martini, Wädenswil.) Winemakers throw the terms around almost reflexively, blissfully unaware that they mean nothing to most everyone outside the wine industry.

While distinct clones display different characteristics—earlier ripening, smaller berries, thicker skins, larger crops—they are all still Pinot Noir. They resemble identical twins who might look the same and have the exact same DNA, but still have different personalities. Pinot has more clonal diversity than any other variety, owing to its inherent genetic instability. Since grape vines can be reproduced asexually by taking a cutting of budwood and either planting it or grafting it to a different rootstock, once an individual grapevine is recognized in a vineyard as having desirable properties it can be isolated and replicated ad infinitum. This is

called "clonal selection." In the environment of contemporary viticulture—and its emphasis on predictability and control—clones are important as they tend to be free of virus and have fairly well understood tendencies.

Today many different clones are available to Pinot growers. Some are divided into sets named according to their provenance. Dijon clones come from selections made by a group from that Burgundian city; Pommard clones reputedly come from Burgundy's Chateau de Pommard; Wädenswil clones, seen mostly in Oregon, come from the town of the same name in Switzerland; and there are many so-called "heritage" clones that have been isolated from older California vineyards, e.g. Calera, Martini, Swan, Pisoni. Tony Soter isolated such a vine while working in California and has now planted his Oregon vineyard to what will become known as the Soter clone. There are also the dark and mysterious "suitcase clones," which refer to budwood brought into this country illegally (meaning that it hasn't been cleared by the government), perhaps swathed in some dirty undergarments in a traveler's suitcase.

On the other hand, winegrowers more interested in diversity

than control might choose to take cuttings from many vines of an old vineyard and replant them in a new site, replicating the entire vineyard. This is called a "mass selection." While this more dated method is not nearly as prevalent today as the targeted planting of various clones, I hear more and more winegrowers talking about using mass selection, as they look for ways to make their vineyards unique in a world where everyone has access to the same plant material.

However, the character of wines produced by the same clone will be different depending on the climate and soils on which they're grown. Therefore, almost every winemaker will tell you that site trumps clone in terms of its influence on a wine. And, much less talked about than clone is rootstock, the subterranean base of a grapevine. Like clones, there are various kinds of rootstock available to growers, each with different skills—some are drought resistant, some are low-vigor, etc. The importance of rootstock, says Adam Lee of Siduri, cannot be underestimated. "After all, a much greater proportion of the vine lives underground than above. And we still know so little about that."

The grapes are long since harvested and the first signs of winter descend on Pinot vineyards just north of Sebastopol in Sonoma's Green Valley appellation next to Russian River.

Sorting fruit at Lemelson Vineyards.

FROM GRAPE TO WINE

MOST VINTNERS WILL SAY THAT 90% of wine-making is done in the vineyard. They like to suggest that their job consists of simply opening the winery door so that the Pinot Noir grapes can saunter into tanks and ultimately tuck themselves into the bottles. It's a good line, both a clever ploy for winemakers to absolve themselves of responsibility if anything goes wrong and a way to seem admirably humble and gracious. But it is also, in a sense, true.

One thing that makes wine compelling is that it is a fundamentally natural product—an invention not of human beings but of nature. Thanks to the ambient yeasts omnipresent in our atmosphere, grapes picked and lightly crushed to release their juice will ultimately turn themselves into wine. That wine will not, most likely, be great, but it will nonetheless be wine. The winemaker's job is to guide and control this natural process so that it results in something delicious.

Any winemaker will tell you that his job is made infinitely easier by starting with top quality grapes, indeed that it is impossible to make good wine without good grapes. However, contrary to the assertion that

Anthony Van Nice of Four Graces sorts clusters at N.W. Wine Company's custom winemaking facility in McMinnville, Oregon.

"The wine just makes itself," the winemaker's job, just as the viticulturist's, is fraught with many, many choices. Each choice leads to a more complicated choice, leaving an infinitely branching chain of causation. Navigating that complex chain is another way to describe the winemaker's job. This is true for all wines, but of course Pinot Noir is special.

Another way of describing the Pinot maker's job might be "innkeeper" or perhaps "spa technician." For hearing the winemaker's description of the job is to hear someone who sounds terribly afraid of offending honored guests—guests who are not grapes to be ruthlessly processed into wine, but spoiled celebrities who want only green M&Ms and flat Perrier in their dressing rooms. "Gentle treatment is a must," says Bob Cabral of Williams Selyem Winery. "Pinot is so sensitive and specific in its needs that rough handling at any point can ultimately show up in the finished wine." What's next, a mani-pedi? Practically.

Pinot Noir, when harvested by any quality producer, is picked by hand. After a year of nurturing and protecting the grapes on the vine, risking the integrity of their delicate, thin skins by machine harvesting is unthinkable. Grapes are picked into and transported to the winery in small bins—the cushy Cadillacs of the wine world—so

Shoveling dry ice on top of freshly sorted grapes at Bergstrom Winery.

that the weight of the lot doesn't damage or crush any grapes on the bottom.

Pinot Noir wineries are often built on levels to accommodate a process of "gravity flow," so that in the interest of gentleness the juice never has to be pumped mechanically from one location to another. Many wineries, such as Penner-Ash, Calera and Domaine Drouhin, are built on several levels of a hillside. In smaller wineries, gravity can be exploited by simply lifting bins or tanks up with forklifts. It's rare that one sees this kind of madness at Cabernet or Syrah houses. Only for Pinot Noir's comfort do the winemakers so bend over backwards.

PRE-FERMENTATION

WINEMAKERS TALK ABOUT THE NECESSITY of beginning fermentation with fruit of good quality. What exactly does that mean? I ask the Oregon winemaker, Ken Wright. "You know good fruit when you see it," he says. "It's just like when you're shopping for apples or bananas at the grocery. You want clean, ripe grapes that are not bruised, broken, moldy or raisined. Any sort of imperfection of the grapes can open the door for the kind of spoilage bacteria that can ruin a fermentation." For this reason, Wright and most Pinot producers employ sorting tables and teams

Adam and Dianna Lee of Siduri winery use their feet to stomp down cap inside fermentation tank.

"Free run" juice (before grapes are pressed) pours out of fermentation tank showcasing gentle winemaking.

Punchdown at Flowers Vineyard on the Sonoma Coast.

A French turbo pigeur used at Flowers Vineyard to gently pump over the fermentating must.

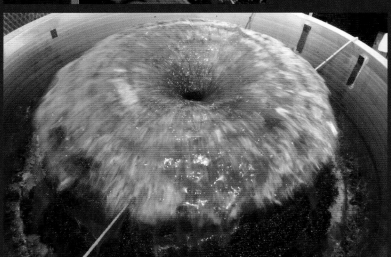

of sorters that go through the Pinot cluster by cluster, sometimes grape by grape, as it comes from the vineyards and goes into the tank. Each year, Wright fields a team of volunteers to work hours in quality control, braving not just the trance-like state that comes from watching millions of grapes pass their eyes, but also any vineyard critters that have to be sorted out.

The next choice is whether to take the grapes off their stems. Machines rather violently called crusher-destemmers stand waiting at most wineries. Using whirling paddles, the machines can be set to crush the grapes a little while separating them from their stems or to leave them whole. Most producers who destem choose to leave some portion of the grapes whole and uncrushed. Because the sweet grape juice remains protected inside the whole grapes (until the skins are punctured or break down), fermentations will begin more gradually.

"Having the grapes come in at the right temperatures is also really important," adds Lynmar's Hugh Chapelle, and by the "right temperature" he means he likes them cold. "We pick very early in the morning to get the grapes at their coolest," he says, "so they go into the cold-soak period as cool as possible." A soak? After the long journey to the winery and all that sorting, it's time for the grapes, naturally, to relax a little. And nothing's more relaxing than a good soak in the tub.

Pre-fermentation maceration, known more colloquially as "cold soak," is practiced by almost every Pinot Noir producer in North America. Though the length of time, usually three to five days,

Handful of fermenting grapes.

Shoveling out excess must from fermentation tank, a job often given to the "lucky" harvest interns.

varies from winery to winery, the practice of letting grapes sit with their skins at a temperature—not too hot, not too cold!—just below what's necessary for fermentation to begin is quite basic. "Cold soak," says Williams Selyem winemaker Bob Cabral, "is all about extracting the color and flavor from the skins using just the water that's in the grapes. Water is a much less aggressive solvent than alcohol, making for an exceedingly gentle extraction." With the beginning of alcoholic fermentation, of course, things get a little more intense for the grapes.

FERMENTATION

WHEN THE WINEMAKER HAS DECIDED that the grapes have had enough of a cold soak, it's time for (what else?) the hot tub party also known as fermentation. As winemakers gradually allow the vat of grapes and juice—called the "must"—to warm, fermentation is ready to begin. The winemaker here must make a big decision. Besides the Pinot Noir, who to invite to this party? There are two choices of guests: the ambient yeasts that arrive on the grape skins and live in the winery, or a commercially isolated species of yeast that the winemaker selects. Both schools have their adherents.

The argument in favor of adding yeast to conduct the fermentation involves the desire to control—the winemaker can select a preferred strain of yeast that will finish the job in a predictable manner. This kind of party is like a high school dance: fun, but orderly.

A basket press is used to extract juice from the must at Flowers Vineyard and Winery.

"Pinot noir is the most challenging grape. It's like dealing with . . . I don't want to sound sexist, but, you know what I mean . . . It does the opposite of everything you think it's going to do. It's got its own mind. For that Pinot's the ultimate challenge. But it's also the ultimate nirvana."

Ambient yeasts are unpredictable; you never know whom you're getting. Consequently, the party is more diverse and wild—an outdoor rock concert, perhaps. The advantage of diversity is complexity in the finished wine. As many, many species of wild yeast do their part, each produces different compounds as it converts the grapes' sugars into alcohol. But just as at any party, if you don't control the guest list, you might end up with some undesirables carrying on and the whole thing could go sour.

Some winemakers hedge their bets. Mark Vlossak of St. Innocent adds a tiny bit of commercial yeast into one corner of his fermenting tank (a sort of chaperone?), while the rest of the tank is allowed to start on its own. The two kinds of yeasts duke it out in the tank, though it might not be much of a contest—the commercial strains are severely outnumbered. "I don't know if it even makes a difference that I put that yeast in there," he concedes, "but it just makes me feel better."

Fermentation can last from three or four days up to a week. Like any good party, Pinot fermentations like to get hot. Winemakers exert a measure of control over this by using temperature-controlled tanks. If it's cool enough tanks can be just moved outside to ferment in the cool night air. Cooler and slower fermentations prolong the process and make for more subtle, thorough extraction of color, flavor and tannin from the grapes. But every winemaker has his or her style. Jim Prosser of Oregon's J.K. Carriere winery, for instance, says he expressly lets his fermentations get warmer than most people's, because he believes it "burns off excess fruit." Whether or not this is true, one can't argue with his wines, which are delicious.

The by-product of fermentation, besides alcohol, is carbon dioxide, which as it rises to escape, pushes all the grape skins and seeds to the top of the vat, forming a hard layer of matter called the "cap." The source of most of a red wine's color and flavor, the skins need to be kept in contact with the juice. The cap must therefore frequently be broken up and mixed back into the juice. Within hours it will re-form and once again be floating on top. The two primary methods of mixing cap and juice are "pumping over" and "punching down." The latter is the traditional style of Burgundy and is practiced by most producers in the United States. Many have pneumatic punchdown devices, such as WillaKenzie Estate's "Bigfoot"—a metal plunger that runs on a rail above each of the tanks—that typically breaks up the cap a few times a day. Mechanical punchdown devices are quite common nowadays and, besides being laborsaving are also stronger and better able to break up the sometimes impenetrable-seeming caps on larger tanks.

However, winemakers dealing with smaller lots, such as Scott Paul Winery's Kelley Fox, prefer to do punchdowns by hand. "Not only would there be a significant loss of important information without that human connection (the smells, the feeling of the cap, etc.)," she says, "but also a metaphysical loss of connection that could only be achieved between two living systems. I know some who would even say using a punchdown tool is much less ideal than using the body itself!" Indeed, Rhys Vineyards of California performs all its punchdowns by foot.

Some producers, however, do not punch down at all. Wells Guthrie of Sonoma's Copain pumps juice from the bottom of the tank back over the top of the cap. He doesn't do this out of laziness, but because he feels the wine he wants to make doesn't require all the extraction that comes from churning the skins.

Still another, newer method is employed at Benton-Lane. A giant bubble of air is created at the base of the tank. As it rises to the top to escape, it breaks and turns over the cap.

Rollin Soles, winemaker at Argyle winery, fills barrels from freshly fermented juice.

French oak barrels being made at Demptos in Napa Valley.

POST FERMENTATION

WHEN FERMENTATION IS FINISHED and all the sugar has been converted to alcohol, the wine (now dry) is drained off the skins, which are then pressed to extract remaining liquid and then discarded (often turned into compost). The wine is then sent to barrel. Good barrels are like fine bed linens: The wines are put in them to rest, and the better quality the wood, the better the wine feels when it is taken out.

As aging vessels, oak barrels offer many benefits. First and foremost, the porousness of the wood allows for the gradual transpiration of oxygen into the wine, helping it become rounder over time.

Beyond that, the kind of wood and how it's treated affect the wine's flavor. The kind and style of barrel are important considerations for the wine. New or used? French oak, American or other? The tradition is that the insides of the barrels are toasted (since fire is used to heat the wood so it can be bent), which caramelizes the wood. A higher level of toasting imparts more roasted, sweet flavors. Lighter toast allows for more direct expression of the oak flavors and tannins. Every winemaker has his preference for toast level.

Most Pinot Noir producers use French oak exclusively, with a medium level of toast. Typically about 30-40% of the total number of barrels used each year are new. Many producers employ a selection

Winemaker Mark Vlossak using nitrogen pressure racking device to gently rack the wine out of barrel into tank at St. Innocent's underground barrel room.

of different coopers, as each one produces barrels with certain qualities—subtlety, sweetness, spice, etc. Citing complexity, some winemakers use up to a dozen different coopers. On the other hand, Hugh Chapelle of Lynmar focuses on two core coopers and has a few odd barrels lying around. "Most winemakers go through a stage where they're enamored of barrels and they can't get enough of coopers and toast levels," he says. "I've kind of been through that and would rather spend more time in the vineyard. I like having two core coopers that set the stage and a few other various things as a spice rack." And then there's the rare winemaker like Patricia Green of Oregon's Patricia Green Cellars, who uses only one kind of barrel, made by a French cooper called Cadus. "I just like the way my wine tastes out of Cadus," she says unapologetically. "You can't taste the new wood at all. There's a gentleness that comes to the wines from these barrels." I can't argue with her, as her wines have that lovely quality of not showing the barrel at all, proving the rule that the best oak barrel—old, new, French or otherwise—is the one you can't taste.

The amount of time a wine spends in barrel is likewise up to the vintner. That time can be as little as ten or eleven months or as long as two years. Winemakers make this decision according to their opinion of the readiness of the wine and to the logistical requirements of their winery. Most winemakers age the wine in barrel for sixteen to eighteen months. Some, however, such as Jim Schulze of California's Windy Oaks, keep certain wines in barrel for up to twenty-five months. "I just taste it and taste it until I decide it's finally ready to come out," says Schulze of his reserve Pinot. "And it usually takes about that long."

The final decision before bottling is whether to filter the wine. Filtration removes any last particles,

Pinot Noir lab analysis at Dobbes Family Estate, Dundee, Oregon.

yeasts or otherwise dangerous substances that could affect the stability of the wine in bottle. While in theory filtering sounds like a good idea, most Pinot producers argue that filtration strips something essential from the wine, so they don't do it (or say that they don't). Others, of course, prefer safety over all and lightly filter their wines.

When it's time for the Pinot Noir to head out into the world as a full-fledged wine, we come to the final step, bottling. A decidedly unromantic, businesslike affair (much like checking out from a hotel) bottling is all about detail, making sure bottles, corks (or screwcaps), and wine are all clean and prepared to travel. After all this lavish treatment, the wine should be looking and feeling great.

Debates in Fermentation

WHOLE CLUSTER OR DESTEMMED?

— Not long ago, few producers would even think about leaving the grapes on their stems during fermentation. The reasons were persuasive: "We can't get the stems ripe and I don't want any green, 'stemmy' flavors ruining the wine," they would say. Indeed a stemmy wine is not attractive. Herbaceous, vegetal and tannic, a wine poorly made with stems is something to be avoided. And so most winemakers did.

Today, however, all this is changing, and it's hard to find Pinot producers who are not at least experimenting with fermenting some percentage of their grapes on the stems. This is called "whole-cluster fermentation," and is the most traditional method of winemaking, since wine was being made long before the advent of the mechanical crusher-destemmer.

U.S. practitioners of whole-cluster fermentation have historically been few in number. An early devotee was Josh Jensen of Calera, who has made wine with stem inclusion his entire career. Steve Dorner of Cristom brought the technique to Oregon, when he came there after having been winemaker at Calera in the early '90s. Along the way, other fervent believers came along, including Brewer-Clifton and Arcadian, both of California. Still

whole-cluster fermentation is a controversial practice even in Burgundy, where a minority of producers practice it full-on (though those producers happen to be many of Burgundy's most esteemed: Domaine de la Romanée Conti, Domaine Leroy and Domaine Dujac, to name a few).

Blending at Siduri.

If you've ever tasted any of those Burgundies or a mature Calera or Cristom, you have experienced the loveliness of a whole-cluster Pinot Noir. Those wines have some qualities that can only be derived from stem inclusion: a uniquely lacey texture, aromas of spices and healthy gardens, and a seductive fullness in the mouth.

There are many theories as to

why the inclusion of stems might help the wines. One is that putting the grapes into tank while still on the stems means that the grapes are not getting crushed at all. Steve Doerner of Cristom agrees that "Whole cluster is the gentlest on the grapes. Nothing happens until the grapes are broken. It allows for a slow, long gradual fermentation. As we're punching down we're breaking grapes slowly, and that, I believe, helps give us that complexity." The preservation of the whole grapes means that fermentation actually begins within each berry. "Instead of one big fermentation," says Joe Davis of Arcadian, "you start out with millions of little ones. This also adds complexity."

The stems can also contribute compounds of tannin that the Pinot Noir grape doesn't have, thus broadening the texture and dimension of the finished wine. "Texturally, stems give the wine some framework, some texture and some soul that you can't get any other way. It also provides some spice and a lot of complexity," says Greg Brewer of Brewer-Clifton and Melville wineries, in California's Sta. Rita Hills. As North American Pinot Noir continues to improve, a small part of it might be because winemakers are using not just the grapes, but also the stems that hold them together

WOODEN FERMENTERS — Most of the fermentation tanks found in American wineries are made of stainless steel. Steel tanks have everything going for them: They're consistent, their temperature is easily controlled, and they're extremely hygienic and easy to clean. Yet more and more producers are interested in going back to wooden fermenters, the kind used way back when.

Why this retro interest? St. Innocent's Mark Vlossak, who has several large wooden fermenters, explains his thinking. "The first thing I was intrigued by was the statements of some Burgundians I met who said they always prefer fermenting in wood. So I bought a couple to try them out."

Vlossak says he then would take grapes harvested from the same vineyard plots at the same time and ferment half in steel and the other half in wood. After the wines had rested in wood a while, he would offer people comparative tastings. "Almost every single person preferred the wood. They would say the wines were more complex and more nuanced. They were sometimes not as fruity, but were always more interesting." Now he puts his best grapes into the wooden fermenters and from those lots selects his best four barrels. That wine becomes his Special Selection Series, sold only as a future with only ninety-eight cases made.

Other wineries, such as Broadley, DeLoach and Archery Summit, are equally enthusiastic about wooden fermenters. The reasons they're so successful are not well understood, except that the wood may be a better insulator than stainless steel, thus making for more consistent fermentations. Also the wood imparts a measure of oxygen into the fermentation, which the yeasts need. "You just have to make sure the tanks are very clean," says Vlossak. "Wood is an organic product and you don't want anything growing in there during the off-season."

Blending at DeLoach Vineyards.

Blending Pinot Noir at ZD Winery.

Mike Eyres, Brian Irvine and Harry Peterson-Nedry compare notes while choosing best barrel blends at Chehalem winery.

Paul Hobbs takes barrel samples at his eponymous winery.

"Pinot Noir can be a sort of mirror. Don't try to make it into something it doesn't want to be, and make wines that you yourself like the taste of. Only if you're true to yourself and true to the Pinot Noir you grow will you have a shot at real success."

—BOB CABRAL, WILLIAMS SELYEM

Bottling and packing A to Z wines at Rex Hill.

Russian River barrel tasting weekend at DeLoach Vineyards.

IN THE GLASS

I T'S NOT DIFFICULT TO ENJOY A GLASS OF GOOD PI-
NOT NOIR. What can be challenging, however, is
getting to the point where you can thirstily take
that initial sip and feel the pleasure centers of your
brain light up like a pinball machine as the silky red
liquid flows across your tongue and down the throat.
Several things must happen first, and each one requires
some informed decision-making. Initially, a bottle must
be selected and procured. The proper time to drink a
wine must be decided upon, as well as the vessel from
which to drink it. And, finally, a decision must be made
as to the food—if any—that will accompany the Pinot.
A wine can benefit from its context, or it can suffer. You
want to give it—and yourself—the best chance for success by making the proper calls each step of the way.

HOW MUCH TO PAY?

GOOD PINOT NOIR ISN'T CHEAP. The economics of the
market dictate that a high quality bottle of Pinot Noir
will not be appearing in your local supermarket's bargain bin any time soon.

Lemelson tasting room in the Dundee Hills.

ton.) A ton of grapes makes about 720 bottles of wine, so the grape cost of good Pinot in Sonoma is just over $5.50 a bottle. Then factor in the costs of winemaking, oak barrels, bottles, corks, labels, storage, taxes, sales and marketing, and salaries. Oh, and tack on a few extra bucks, as the winery would probably like to make a little profit for its year of hard work. The sum of all these costs can easily push a bottle's price from $10 to past $20—and that's wholesale. Traditionally, retailers will mark up that wholesale cost by 50%, and restaurants will mark up a wine at 200% or more.

All this means that if you can find a bottle of good Pinot Noir for less than $20 a bottle, it's coming from smart, talented producers who probably aren't making huge margins on their wines. And these wines are out there: Saintsbury "Garnet" Pinot Noir, A to Z Oregon Pinot, Calera's Central Coast bottlings, to name a few. But these are also each of those wineries' lightest and simplest wines. For my money, it's in the $35–60 range to get to anything that I would consider putting in my cellar for any length of time.

Why? Well, it's quite simple. As an article about the 2007 harvest in the trade publication *Wines & Vines* stated succinctly, "Wineries wanted Pinot Noir more badly than any other major wine variety." Consider that the kind of land needed to grow high quality Pinot Noir is scarce, and thus expensive. And now consider that Pinot Noir is a low-yielding, difficult-to-farm, hand-harvested grape grown on scarce and expensive land. You begin to get the picture.

Without getting out our slide rules, let's sketch out the cost of a bottle made in, say, Sonoma County. Winemakers tell me that the price of quality Pinot grapes these days is around $4,000 per ton. (The 2007 top price for a ton of Pinot in Sonoma County was $11,464. By way of contrast, the most expensive Zinfandel grapes were almost half that at $5,884 per

ARE SINGLE-VINEYARD PINOTS BETTER THAN REGIONAL WINES?

THAT'S A GOOD QUESTION, as there is a raft of single-vineyard bottlings to choose from, and the numbers seem to rise every year. The easy answer is that single-vineyard wines are not always better, though they should be. They are, however, always more expensive.

As Pinot Noir is the grape of Burgundy, our production model for it in the U.S. tends structurally to be Burgundian. That structure dictates that wines blended from diverse, non-contiguous sources should be considered inherently inferior to wines that come from a single superior plot. This thinking derives from belief in

Memorial Day weekend tasting at Adelsheim winery, Yamhill-Carlton.

the concept of terroir, whose apotheosis is experienced in wine that comes solely from one superlative vineyard. Such a wine is deemed inherently more special than one that is cobbled together from numerous and ostensibly inferior vineyards.

But here's the rub: In Burgundy, the single vineyards have been scrutinized, evaluated and ranked for centuries. Indeed, these rankings are now overseen and regulated by the government. The best vineyards have by consensus been agreed upon. Truly lesser vineyards don't even get names; they just produce wines that become part of a blend.

Here in the U.S., not only do we have no such oversight, but more than half of the Pinot vineyards are fewer than ten years old. By my clock, this hasn't exactly given us much perspective on which plots

consistently make better, more age-worthy or otherwise more distinctive wines. That is, it may be too soon to tell which plots are worthy of single-vineyard designation and the typical price hikes that come with it. So caveat emptor on that one.

WHEN TO DRINK IT?

THE FIRST QUESTION TO ASK YOURSELF before sentencing any bottle to years in the cellar is, "Do I like older wines?" Many people store wines reflexively with the belief that this is how wine should be treated. This, however, is not the case. The aging of quality wines can have a couple of effects. Over time, the wine's primary fruit flavors will diminish and

Tasting patio at Alma Rosa Winery, Sta. Rita Hills, California.

be replaced with savory note—spice, leather, meat, tea—its color will fade, and its aromas will become more complex. If you like these qualities—and I certainly do—you might consider putting some of your better bottles in temperature-controlled storage (55-60°F is desirable) for anywhere from three to ten years.

It should be noted that Pinot Noir—especially New World Pinot—is generally regarded as a wine that's good to drink young, and most winemakers purposefully make their wine in a style that allows for early drinking. Producers who make their wines

specifically for the long haul are few and far between. To be sure that a wine you've purchased has the necessary concentration and balance to evolve evenly and gracefully, it's always wise to consult the knowledgeable merchant you bought it from or, better yet, to get the opinion of the winery.

One note on the subject of young wines: I have noticed a tendency for many West Coast Pinots to fall into a "dumb phase" in their youth. It often happens about a year after release (two to three years after the vintage date) and can last for up to a year or two, but rarely longer. In this state,

Food and wine pairing at Lynmar Estate.

the wine isn't bad, just slightly disappointing, with muted aromas and flavors. The experience is of feeling the weight of the wine in the mouth, but tasting very little. To avoid this, I like to either drink the wines squarely in their infancy or let them get a few years into maturity before opening them.

DO VINTAGES MATTER?

VINTAGES ARE SOMEWHAT LIKE HAIRCUTS. While hair can be sculpted in vastly different ways to create vastly different looks, it's always the same hair. The same can be said of vintages. Depending on the conditions of the year, wines may have distinctly different characteristics. In a low-crop year, a wine can be like a buzz cut—very little of it is available. In some years, however, it can be quite copious like my ancestors' hair from the 1970s. Yet despite its length and shape, a wine from a given place will

Chehalem's tasting room in Newberg, Oregon.

Horseback riding with Equestrian Wine Tours through Stoller Vineyards, Dundee Hills, Oregon.

always remain essentially itself. The major difference between vintages and haircuts is that winegrowers have much less control over the outcome than, say, my stylist, Nikki, has over my sideburns.

Oregon is often cited as the place that's prone to significant differences from vintage to vintage, while conversely, it's not uncommon to hear people blow off the idea of vintage variation in California. However, nothing could be further from reality. Not only does Oregon have excellent vintages with much greater consistency than conventional wisdom has given it credit for, but there is also significant vintage variation in California. In fact, in any given year there's often tremendous variation among different parts of the Golden State. Rarely, for instance, do the northern regions of Sonoma and Mendocino have comparable conditions to vineyards down in Santa Barbara County.

How does this affect you? Well, only as much as you want it to. One of the traits of modern winemaking is that very good wines can still be made in even the most difficult of vintages. Good vintages will always have an advantage over poor ones. For most top-notch winemakers, the hallmark of a bad vintage will be reduced quantity, not significantly lower quality. "I'll sacrifice as much fruit as I need to in order to make good wine," says Ehren Jordan of Failla, based in the Sonoma Coast region. "It's always painful to see your crop whittled down, but with Pinot especially high quality takes precedence over everything."

For questions of when to drink, how long to

Enjoying a private wine tasting at the Four Graces vineyard patio, Dundee, Oregon.

age and sometimes even what to serve with any given wine, the vintage can matter. But, no matter the fineness of the haircut, a person of character will always continue to be himself. And the same is true of wine. I celebrate, rather than fear, vintage variation. Indeed, it's one of the pleasures of a good Pinot Noir that it can sport a slightly different look from year to year, but still be essentially itself.

WHAT TO DRINK IT OUT OF?

MUCH FUN HAS BEEN MADE of the propensity of wine connoisseurs to require a specific glass in order to drink a certain variety. Indeed, many articles have been written in the service of debunking this perception. As a 2004 article in *Gourmet* put it, "Despite . . . claims—and despite all the anecdotal testimony from wine critics and consumers alike—researchers haven't found any scientific evidence that a $90 glass makes your wine smell or taste better than a $3 version from Wal-Mart . . . studies suggest you've been brainwashed."

If I'm brainwashed, please make no attempt to rehabilitate me. While Pinot Noir can certainly be enjoyed from any vessel, I believe that the rotund and squat Pinot "bowl" is far and away the best shape of glass from which to drink it. In fact, its ability to deliver the complexity and dimensionality of a fine, mature Pinot Noir is nothing short of miraculous.

I asked Georg Riedel, whose family's famous glassmaking company came up with the original Pinot glass design, how it came about. It was, he said, "by accident, by serendipity." The shape was not engineered, but discovered, almost like a new species or new star in the firmament. Georg's father, Claus Riedel, came up with the design for "aesthetic reasons at the behest of a friend from Italy's Piedmont region," Riedel told me. "The customer said he was tired of drinking Barolo from such a small glass. My father worked to design something much bigger and more beautiful, and the basic shape of the Pinot Noir glass came about."

It was only later and over the years, Riedel said, that the glass was found to suit Pinot Noir perfectly. Now the basic bowl-shaped design is employed in various iterations by Riedel in no fewer than nine of its glasses, as well as by most other glassware companies.

With the help of a panel of Oregon winemakers, Riedel even designed a glass specifically for that state's Pinot Noir. Its basic shape is consistent with the classic Pinot bowl, but it narrows a little more at the top before flaring at the rim. "Truly, the shape is different from our other Pinot Noir glasses," Riedel enthuses. "And it does accentuate the particularities of Oregon Pinot Noir in a very special way. But there's no (scientific) reason for it." I can agree that the glass does work wonderfully for Oregon Pinot, but my own testing found that it's not too shabby with Pinot from other places, either.

Private lunch at Soter's new winery in Carlton, Oregon, features local produce and special wine pairings.

International Pinot Noir Celebration's traditional salmon bake in the lantern-lit Oak Grove on Linfield campus, McMinnville, Oregon.

Winemakers technical tasting at Steamboat Pinot Noir Conference in southern Oregon. This intensive international producers' seminar began in 1980 as a way to improve the overall quality of Pinot Noir with open, frank, constructive conversations following blind tastings of paticipants' wines.

Riedel agrees with *Gourmet* insofar as he emphasizes that there is no existing scientific way to test that the shape of the Pinot glass objectively improves the experience of the wine. "We only have the tens of thousands of people who choose this shaped glass to drink their Pinot Noir. I believe Pinot Noir is a grape that carries enormous complexity and has enormous varieties of presentations. If you look at all the places it comes from and all the expressions of the grape, there is a worldwide orchestra of Pinot Noirs which at the end of the day all fit into one glass. And this is the DNA of the Pinot Noir grape."

WHAT TO DRINK IT WITH?

PINOT NOIR IS CONSIDERED TO BE the most food friendly of red wine grapes, and for good reason. What makes it such a utility player? Like a devout Buddhist, it follows the middle path. Relative to other red wines, most Pinots are medium bodied, moderately tannic, have good acidity and are natively complex. This allows Pinot Noir to reach up to pair with lighter foods or reach down to be a good match with heavier ones. While few would dare drink Cabernet with fish, Pinot Noir can be as good a match as many a white wine. I've had American Pinot Noir with *toro* (fatty tuna) at one of Tokyo's finest sushi restaurants. Yet I've also enjoyed Pinot in big-red country: with a nice steak, grilled rare, in Argentina. It's even worked favorably for me with Brussels sprouts.

But after that, it's a question of shading. For more perspective, I talked to Rajat Parr, a sommelier by trade. Parr also happens to be a trained chef who graduated at the top of his class at the Culinary Institute of America and now produces his own California Pinot Noir. As wine director for the plethora of restaurants across the country owned by the Michael Mina group, Parr is also regarded as the possessor of one of the world's finest palates. So who better to provide a Pinot perspective?

Pairing food with Pinot Noir, says Parr, when I ask him for some ideas, "can get pretty geeky, because you can think of what you can have with different areas and even different vintages."

"Get geeky," I encourage.

"Okay," he says, taking a deep breath. "If I create a mental grid of Pinot pairing, I narrow it down. First I look for basic fruit flavors. Then, in another square, I put acid. Then tannin. Then I break down the flavors. Is it smoky? Does it have menthol? Then I do the same thing with the dish. A way to think about the relationship between the two is to ask if there's a certain aspect missing in either the wine or the dish—you can use one to fill in the void in the other. It definitely makes it complicated, especially with Pinot Noir, which for me is a very fruity grape.

"For example, lots of people think salmon works very well with Pinot Noir. I don't think so." (At this, my face turns a little red: I have always loved salmon and Pinot.) "The flavor of salmon can be so oily and pronouncedly fishy, which doesn't often work with Pinot's fruitiness. But you can do swordfish. My favorite is turbot. Tuna tartare can also be great with a delicate, not too complicated Pinot."

Okay, he's getting pretty geeky. Parr goes on to say how much he likes squab dishes and quail with Pinot. Veal chops and pork. Even lobster, if you cook it in red wine. With delicate fish dishes, you need to have a Pinot with very good acidity. And, naturally, mushrooms are a classic Pinot pairing. This reminds me of the Joel Palmer House in Oregon wine country, a restaurant devoted to mushrooms and Pinot. Parr's favorites are portobello, shiitakes and dark wild mushrooms. "The more intense the mushrooms, the more intense the Pinot you need to use."

So, while noting a few personal caveats, Parr's litany backs up the idea of Pinot's remarkable versatility. He leaves me with one tip for the home chef, and it makes a lot of poetic sense. "A good thing with Pinot Noir is to finish a sauce with a tablespoon of whatever you're drinking. It creates a bridge between wine and food that always holds up. I've used some of the great wines of the world like this—just a little bit—and it always works out great. That's why Pinot Noir is the greatest red grape in the world."

A PINOT NOIR ROAD GUIDE

PINOT NOIR SEEMS TO INSPIRE FANATICAL PASSION more than any other wine. This is evident in the sheer number of festivals and publications devoted to this one grape. I don't see the same level of commitment in the supporters of, say, Chardonnay or Cabernet Sauvignon, which to my knowledge don't really have their own exclusive publications and celebrations. With that in mind, next time you want to celebrate Pinot Noir with a large, riotous group of like-minded individuals, here are some of your choices of venue.

Mushrooms pair perfectly with Pinot Noir at Lynmar Estate in Russian River, Sonoma.

Wild salmon is prepared Northwest style on alder stakes over a huge custom-built fire pit.

INTERNATIONAL PINOT NOIR CELEBRATION (IPNC)

THE GRANDDADDY OF THEM ALL, IPNC debuted in 1987 and continues to take place at the end of every July in McMinnville, right in the heart of Oregon Pinot Country. While a good bit of the focus is on the local juice, great producers come from around the world to participate in fascinating panel discussions, tastings, meals, tastings, and more tastings. The final night's salmon dinner is always one of the best dinners of the year. It consistently sells out, so get tickets well in advance. www.ipnc.org

¡SALUD!

Every November the Oregon wine industry throws a gala auction to raise money to provide healthcare outreach services for seasonal vineyard workers and their families who cannot qualify for health insurance plans. The focus of the auction is on premium Oregon Pinot Noirs and the benefactors are drawn by the only opportunity to purchase limited production wines from the state's top producers. www.saludauction.org

International Pinot Noir Celebration.

WORLD OF PINOT NOIR

CALIFORNIA'S ANSWER TO IPNC is the World of Pinot Noir, an equally wonderful gathering that takes place at Shell Beach on California's Central Coast. Just rounding out its first decade, WOPN invites Pinot producers from around the world, though emphasis is always placed on the local producers. Seminars, bus tours, meals and tastings make for a relaxing, but jam-packed weekend. The final night's massive party, typically hosted by Au Bon Climat/Qupé winery is both the showstopper and hangover-starter. Early March. www.worldofpinotnoir.com

PINOT DAYS

A MASSIVE, MULTI-DAY PRODUCTION, Pinot Days focuses on the Pinot producers of California. It takes Pinot appreciation to an intense, wonderfully geeky level with winemaker dinners, panel discussions and focused tastings of various vintages and single vineyards. San Francisco in the summer and Chicago in the fall. www.pinotdays.com

Couples enjoy dancing to live music at Willamette Valley Vineyards.

Mark and Ben McWilliams of Arista winery engage with aficionados at Pinot Days in San Francisco.

ANDERSON VALLEY PINOT NOIR FESTIVAL

THE NAME EXPLAINS IT ALL FOR THIS ANNUAL FESTIVAL in and of Mendocino's celebrated Pinot Noir district. Attracting nearly 500 people, the gathering offers a good chance to taste in one setting the diverse wines of a small region. Lodging in the valley is limited, so book early. Usually held the third weekend in May. www.avwines.com

PINOT PARADISE

SO LITTLE PINOT NOIR IS PRODUCED in the Santa Cruz Mountains, that it's understandable to fear that it may all be slurped up over the two days of this local festival. Held at the Mountain Winery (formerly Paul Masson) in Saratoga, it's one of the best ways to sample the wines from this very exciting region. Usually held in the second half of March. www.scmwa.com

Winery tour at the Robert Mondavi Winery.

View from Hanzell's historic winery.

"Pinot Noir, more than anything, should tell the truth. And it does that very well. But you have to take a risk in order to hear the truth and then you might not always hear what you expect."

—SCOTT WRIGHT, SCOTT PAUL WINERY

Riedel's Oregon Pinot glass is designed to enhance the wine's unique characteristics.

ACKNOWLEDGMENTS

PASSION FOR PINOT has been our personal passion for several years. It has been a labor of love that would never has blossomed without the help of our many friends in the Pinot world.

In California: Kris Curran, Paul Hobbs, Brett deLuze, George Rose, Michael Terrien, Bob Cabral, Richard and Tekla Sanford, the McWilliams family, Elan Fayard, Victor Gallegos, Jean-Charles Boisset, Lisa Heisinger, Tia Butts, Steve Myars, Lisa Goff, Ryan Moore, Adam and Diana Lee, Ehren Jordan and Christopher Barefoot.

In Oregon: Ronnie and Bernie Lacroute, Harry Peterson-Nedry, Bill and Cathy Stoller, David Adelsheim, Tony Soter, Lynn and Ron Penner-Ash, Ken and Karen Wright, Mark Vlossak, Tim and Kari Ramey, Jim Bernau, Steve and Carol Gerard, Deb and Bill Hatcher, Steve and Paula Black, Adam Campbell, Anthony King, Heather Belt and Sheila Nicholas.

Thank you, thank you, thank you.

Without the help of Ross Eberman we would still be mired in paperwork. Dick Owsiany ensured that our vision translated onto the page and George Olson's critical eye kept us focused on our best images. We also express our gratitude to Ian, Alan and Usana for their creative design, hard work and patience.

Finally, a huge dept of thanks to Jordan Mackay who put our dream into words with an eloquence and wit that more than lived up to our expectations.

—*Robert Holmes and Andrea Johnson*

While writing the book required many solitary hours, none of it could have been accomplished without the collaboration of many others. Foremost thanks to Bob Holmes and Andrea Johnson for inviting me to be a part of their project. Getting to know them has been a joy, and along the way they were nothing but cheerful, supportive and staunchly protective of my liberty to write only the words I wanted to write. Those words are hardly deserving of sharing the page with the visual splendor that Bob and Andrea captured so beautifully.

Thanks too to the following: Tina Caputo, who logged many hours editing the text; the wonderful Eric Asimov for gracing this book with his words; and the many exceptional producers of Pinot Noir in Oregon and California who shared their time, knowledge and delicious wine.

Thanks also to the Campion family of Carlton, Oregon. Nancy, David and Ashley may have been kind enough to provide me with a place to stay in their home on each of my many research trips to Oregon, but what I am most thankful for is the opportunity to become friends with them, their friends, cats and all the neighborhood dogs.

Thanks also to my dad, Gloria and Moira for being there for me, as well as to Eden, John and Clementine for keeping me going.

Without the crack, last-minute editing by my mother the text of this book would not be nearly as coherent. Any clunky sentences in these acknowledgments are attributable to the fact that she will not see these words until they've already been printed. Thanks so much, Mom.

Most of all, thanks to my wife, Christie Dufault, who has taught me so much about wine and expanded my vinous horizons far more than even she realizes. She also tolerated my inconsistencies, irregular hours and occasional bouts of absent-mindedness and repaid such annoyances with love and support. I am deeply grateful.

What a beautiful planet to give us the Pinot Noir grape.

—*Jordan Mackay*

PHOTO CREDITS

ANDREA JOHNSON

TITLE PAGE, 8–9, 16, 19, 20, 21 BOTTOM, 22–23, 24, 26, 28–29, 30, 31, 33, 36–37, 38, 40, 41, 43, 44–45, 46, 47, 57 TOP, 64, 65, 68–69 OREGON PORTRAITS, 70, 72–73, 74, 75, 76–77, 78 TOP & BOTTOM, 80, 82, 84–85, 86, 88 BOTTOM, 91, 92, 93, 94–95, 96, 97, 98, 99, 102, 103, 106, 107, 111 BOTTOM RIGHT, 116, 117, 118 TOP TWO, 119, 123, 125 TOP, 126, 127, 130, 132, 133, 137, 138, 140, 141, 142, 143, 144–145, 146, 148 RIGHT, 150, 154, 156–157

ROBERT HOLMES

Morning fog retreats from the Calera vineyards on Mount Harlan.

INDEX

Note to readers: Page numbers in **bold** type indicate photographs or their captions.

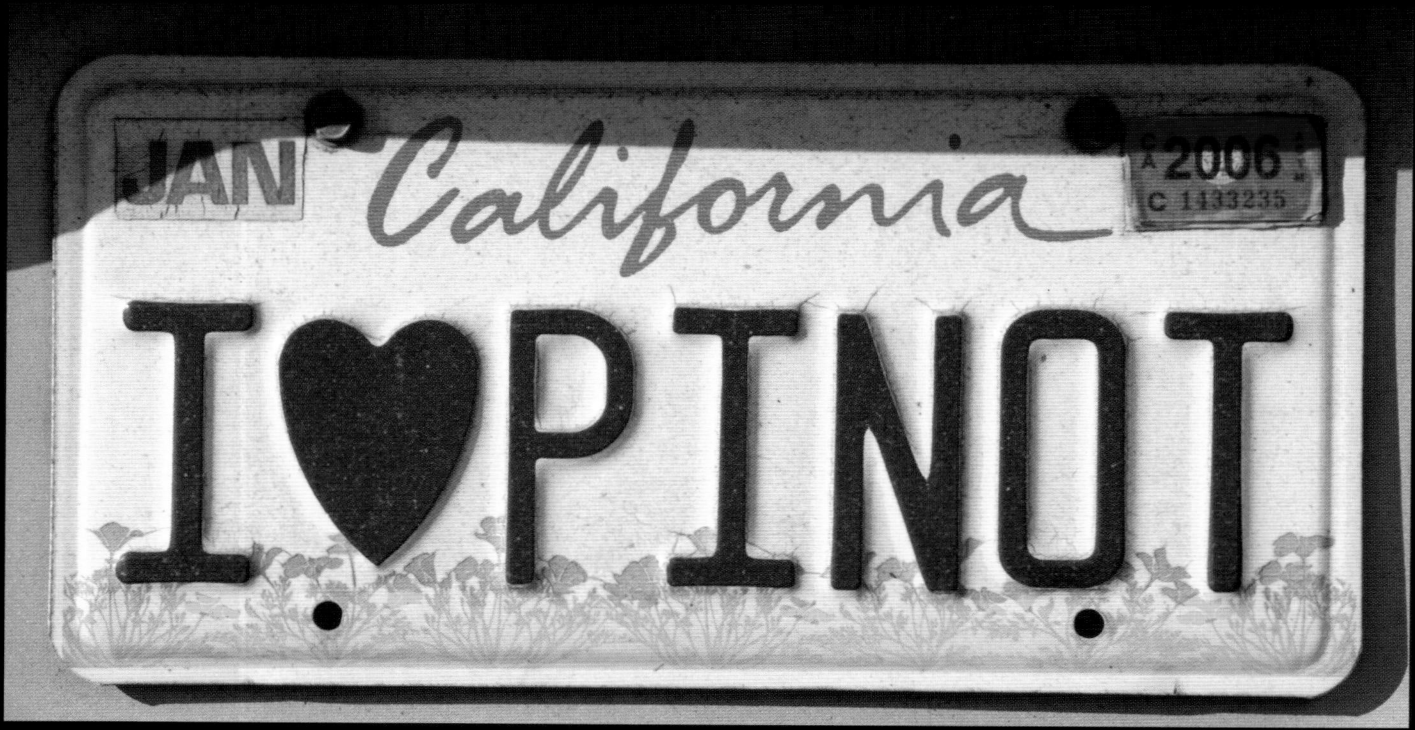
JAN
California
2006
I ♥ PINOT

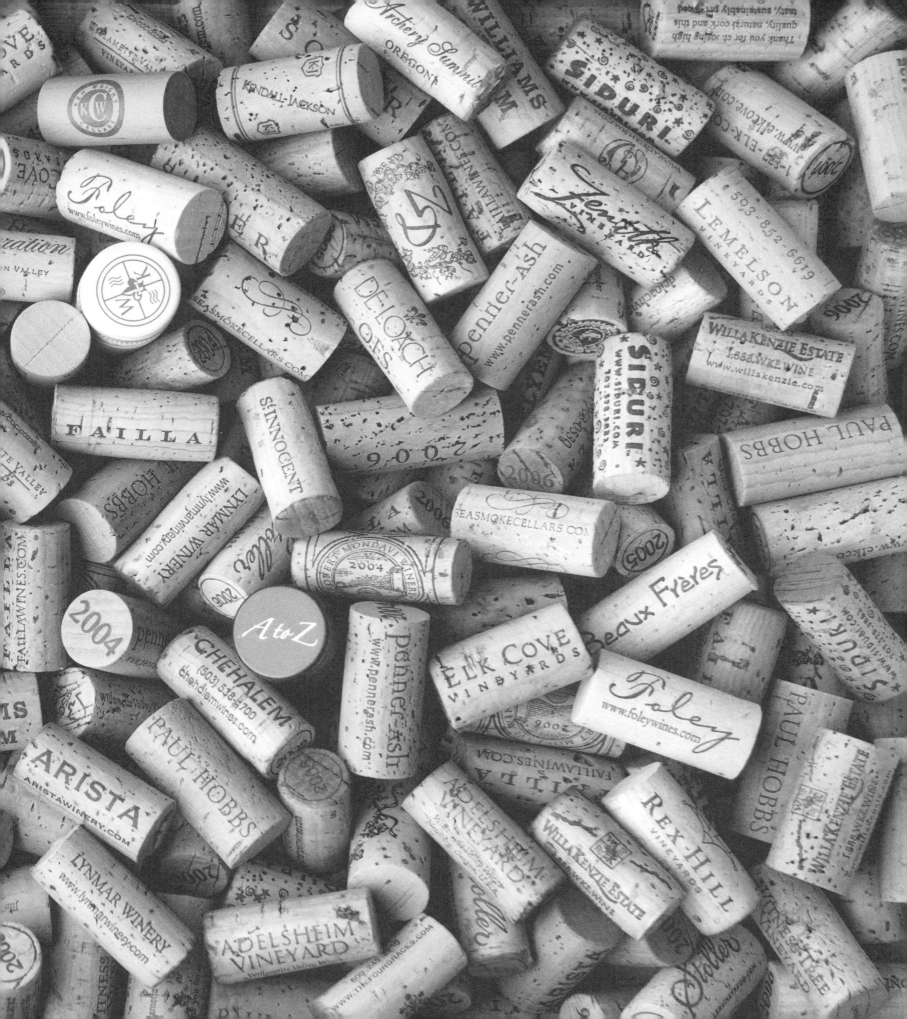